Advance Praise for

Aimless

"John outlines some of the most important aspects of masculinity. By telling his story, he is able to connect with other men struggling with the same problems and offer a solution. Stud!"

—Ryne Ogren, professional baseball player

"*Aimless* masterfully navigates the complexities of being a man. Reading it is truly a transformative experience. It left me with a newfound perspective on vulnerability, trust, and masculinity. I recommend this book to people from all backgrounds, particularly men."

—Sam Deignan, Boston College

"John's stories show us how emotional intelligence and personal growth are not only vital to health and life enjoyment but also essential to top-tier performance."

—Riley Snow, high school senior varsity basketball and golf, National Honor Society member, Special Olympics student board member

"For the longest time, I thought I was the only one going through many of the challenges discussed in *Aimless*. It was an isolation stemming from hollow messaging that, as a man, I have to deal with everything on my own. While

I do have to take ownership of myself and my decisions, opening myself up to others' advice and perspectives has helped keep me on the right path. Allowing others to help me has been indescribably valuable!"

—Goanar Mar, Northern Iowa varsity basketball, first-generation South Sudanese immigrant, and real estate agent

"Of all the books I have ever read, *Aimless* made the deepest connections to my life. Through engaging stories and brutal honesty, *Aimless* is the perfect book for any man looking for guidance toward a fulfilling life."

—Tim Petersen, entrepreneur, Rowan University varsity basketball, and exercise science major

"It felt like *Aimless* had been written about my own life. Many of the struggles John described I too had been through, and many of the emotions he felt I too had felt. The parallels of his story to my own brought me to the realization that many men silently go through the same struggles."

—Lex Cisler, sales executive, survivalist, author, and collegiate athlete

"I learned so many lessons reading *Aimless*, and one lesson that stood out is transparency. In order to be a successful leader and person, you have to be transparent with yourself and others. John upholds this throughout *Aimless*, teaching hugely important lessons through his personal stories and reflections that can change lives."

—Mason Toye, professional soccer player

"*Aimless* provides lessons that create a more holistic person. It talks about topics and issues men have experienced but few are willing to talk about. John helps guide the reader without just telling them explicitly what to do; it feels more like sitting down with a friend discussing life."

—**Noah Roll, Tufts University clinical psychology and community health major**

"*Aimless* is a book that people from all backgrounds can learn from. Throughout *Aimless*, John provides crucial insight and concepts on life that may seem foreign to some (especially men). These concepts are a necessity for men to learn and understand, as they will only become more relevant as our society continues to advance. *Aimless* is a page-turner, and I would highly recommend it to anyone, regardless of their age or status in life."

—**Jack McBride, United States Naval Academy, senior varsity tennis player**

"*Aimless* is a raw, gritty exposé of the modern man's struggle to define and embrace masculinity in a healthy way. Detailed personal experiences and interludes of candid wisdom serve to engage and educate the reader, making this a must-read for all men."

—**Armaan Gori, MIT '20 electrical engineering and computer science major**

Aimless

A Journey to Constructive Masculinity

JOHN D'AGOSTINI

ISBN 13: 978-1-63489-566-8

Library of Congress Catalog Number has been applied for.
Printed in the United States of America
First Printing: 2022

26 25 24 23 22   5 4 3 2 1

Cover design by David Drummond
Interior design by Patrick Maloney

Wise Ink Creative Publishing
807 Broadway St. NE
Suite 46
Minneapolis, MN 55413

Invictus

Out of the night that covers me,
   Black as the pit from pole to pole,
I thank whatever gods may be
   for my unconquerable soul.

In the fell clutch of circumstance
   I have not winced nor cried aloud.
Under the bludgeonings of chance
   My head is bloody, but unbowed.

Beyond this place of wrath and tears
   Looms but the Horror of the shade,
And yet the menace of the years
   Finds and shall find me unafraid.

It matters not how strait the gate,
   How charged with punishments the scroll,
I am the master of my fate:
   I am the captain of my soul.

—William Ernest Henley

In honor of men who serve others.

Contents

Foreword

Over the past decade, I have mentored hundreds of young men in ten major American cities. I have been fortunate to work with a broad range of individuals—juvenile offenders, students, immigrants, professional athletes, Olympians, and many more. You name them, I've worked with them.

My experience has shown me that the most crucial component to successful mentoring is an environment built upon mutual trust. That trust doesn't come cheap. It requires time and patience, and the mentor must be nonjudgmental to help the mentee feel safe. Along with great accomplishment and personal transformation, mentoring allows space for difficult and even sometimes tragic conversations. Mentorship may be the only place where a man feels he can breach certain topics without fear of being judged or shamed.

Over the years, I have had far too many private conversations with men regarding their struggles with toxic masculinity. Interestingly, these struggles were not limited to one group of men. Toxic masculinity reaches across traditional societal barriers, and our experiences mirror one another. However, most men's experiences remain unspoken.

So why aren't men talking? Because that's not what we do. Instead, we abide by a *code of silence*, even at the expense of our own well-being. This book defies that code.

You are about to read many of the most powerful moments of my life. Like many men, I long abided by toxic masculine themes: violence, emotional suppression, and intolerance of women, just to name a few, to the point where they ruined my life. Only with years of reflection and support was I able to abandon those destructive themes and trudge through a long battle with mental illness that was spawned from following toxic male ideologies.

Although toxic masculinity is often an academic pursuit, this book is a collection of short stories paired with reflections. This approach allows readers to digest what are otherwise complicated topics and see them through a life lens. The stories are raw and gritty. You will not find fluff here.

The book starts with the worst day of my life. From there, it ventures into other impactful moments over the course of ten chaotic years. Like many, I didn't learn in a straight line. I got shoved around, and the lessons from one struggle only took root when combined with the lessons from another. The loss experienced in the first chapter forced me to learn from my past and make the sacrifices necessary to build a future. The format of the book reflects that introspection process.

My life did eventually rebound stronger than ever, but only because I was willing to change, and redefine what being a "man" meant to me. My hope is that the reflections in this book will challenge other men to do the same.

The codes of behavior that men are held to are a false metric for success that only lead to problems. In my case they led to isolation, burnout, and mental illness. These beliefs have also destroyed the lives of others and needlessly perpetuated pain onto generations of men *and* women throughout history.

Which is why I wrote this. Too many men are suffering, and too many people are negatively impacted by behaviors aligned to toxic masculinity. Men need to change, grow, and learn how to connect. We need to be more. Only by embracing our humanity and exploring our spirituality can we find hope.

The Worst Day of My Life

2013

Years earlier, my mother unlocked the door and snuck into my room while I was sleeping. It was a rough experience. After that, I took precautions. Every night, I barricaded the door and hid a knife behind my nightstand.

This night, she woke me up by slamming herself against the door. I heard the lock open and saw the handle turn. I got out of bed and grabbed the knife. She usually tired out, but tonight she escalated. She began violently beating the door and screaming threats. She finally quit at 3:00 a.m., but the smell of her rotten booze breath remained. I stood there with the knife in my hand until the sun came up. I was completely numb.

She always slept late, so eventually I knew it was safe to come out. I went through the house and made sure she didn't leave any stove burners lit or the oven on and open. Luckily, she only opened all the drawers and cabinets in the house. She did stuff like this all the time. It used to scare me, but over time it became annoying. I always had to clean up after her.

I walked to her bedroom and pressed my ear to the door but didn't hear anything. I entered and saw that her bed was empty, so I checked the bathroom. There she was, slumped against the wall and passed out on the toilet. Her mouth was open, but she didn't look like she was breathing. I checked for a pulse and found it, which I had mixed feelings about. The first few times I discovered her like this, I carried her to bed and was always concerned that she might not wake up. This time, I left her there and made myself breakfast.

Hours later she came into the kitchen, smiled, and said hello. She asked me what plans I had for the day and if I was having any luck getting job interviews. This had been our routine for years, but it wasn't always this way. We had a wonderful relationship for decades, but now it seemed the first few hours of the day was our only chance to keep it alive. Every day it seemed like the good hours got shorter, and our relationship deteriorated along with her sobriety. She'd start to drink in the early afternoon, then pop pills in the early evening, and by nighttime, she was a monster.

What made this transformation even worse was that she retained every ounce of her brilliant intellect even during her most inebriated moments. It allowed her to be incredibly calculated with no inhibitions or moral compass. She was cruel, manipulative, and sinister. Then she'd wake up and act like nothing ever happened. She even showed me kindness during her sobriety. Her denial was so convincing that it loosened my grip on reality. She had me fully convinced that all the things she did either never happened or were my fault.

The sober hours were still good though. We could talk and laugh freely. I think we both held on to our relationship for this reason. I always felt her drug use made her behavior understandable and in its own way, tolerable. Sadly, her addictions grew. Something had to give. I just never expected us to break while she was sober.

She hadn't even finished her coffee that morning before she started in on me. It caught me completely off guard. Instead of panicking, I slowed down and went completely still. I stared at her and didn't take my focus off her face. Her face would tell me everything.

My heart sank. Our relationship was over. Even in sobriety, her demons had taken full control. She didn't even try to control herself. She showed no hesitation or conscience. She just cut loose on me, detailing every wrong I had ever done while simultaneously threatening my body.

After eight years of drug- and alcohol-ridden abuse and manipulation, it was only during her sobriety that I gave myself permission to make the choice: leave or stay.

I walked away from her shrieking, went upstairs, and packed everything I had into two duffel bags. I carried them outside and loaded them into my car along with my dog. Then I walked back to the front door, steeled myself, and pushed. She was waiting so close to the door that it nearly hit her as I swung it open. She started screaming again, but I didn't listen. I spoke to her very clearly and slowly. Only after I said, "I'm leaving," did she go quiet.

She responded by belittling me, and my blood boiled. I felt inches from violence. I closed my eyes and took a breath.

The rage turned to grief, and I started sobbing.

She looked at me, smiled, and started laughing. I tried to hide my face from her.

"What a pussy," she said.

In that moment, a part of me died. I knew the moment for what it was—the end. I didn't have anything to say to her besides, "I'm sorry. I love you."

She responded, "Burn in Hell."

I walked to my car and drove away.

Those were the last words that my mother and I said to each other.

All I remember—of the next few days or weeks, even—is sleeping in my car with my dog on random side streets where I knew she would never find me. I don't know how long that lasted because I was completely blacked out. Eventually I texted my friend Mike and told him that I needed a place to crash while I got on my feet. His parents, Mr. and Mrs. "C," took me in that same day, no questions asked.

They both greeted me at the door, gave me hugs, and told me that I could stay with them as long as I needed to. All I could say was thank you, and I promised them that I'd get a job as soon as possible to pay them rent while I figured out what to do. They refused the idea and instead focused on me. They wanted to know if I was okay. I told them yes, but despite my best efforts to look okay, I'm sure it was obvious that I was not.

Mrs. C sat me down and tried to understand what was going on, but I wouldn't talk about it. I deflected. Thankfully, she didn't press me. Instead, she told me, **"I know you're a big, strong man JohnnyD, but you're a person too. And people need help sometimes."**

I broke down when she said that. I was so ashamed. All my awards and accomplishments meant nothing. I saw myself as a crying little boy who couldn't hack real life.

We just sat there for a while.

Eventually, Mr. and Mrs. C showed me where I would sleep. The room was spotless, and the bed was made. I could see how much trouble they had gone to, and it made me feel even worse to be such a burden, with my dog too, no less. That night, I couldn't bring myself to dirty the bed, so I slept on the floor. It provided me with a sense of physical safety but also made me feel a sickening self-shame. I thought both were necessary. I curled up next to my dog and listened for the sound of her car in case she found me. I still barricaded the door, and I still had the knife.

Cause for Reflection

This happened hundreds of times over the span of eight years. By the end, I was numb and dead inside. It may be hard to understand, but like many who come into contact with opioids, my mother developed an addiction accidentally. That addiction distorted her brain, invaded our family, and ultimately destroyed our relationship. Since then, it has taken me a decade of reflection, deep thought, and introspection to process her death threats, suicide attempts, and all the other traumatic experiences associated with her decline. She was my hero in every way, but she became a different person as a result of her addictions. Regretfully, so did I.

As much as I changed during those years, I changed even more after reflecting upon them. Only when we *reflect* upon the *source* of our suffering, do we change for the better. We no longer labor under the same delusions that we held prior to our suffering. As a result, our priorities shift, and space is created in our hearts. Reflection allows us to fill that void with compassion for all those who suffer and teaches us to refrain from competing over who "had it worse." Suffering is suffering. Pain is pain. **The details of suffering don't matter nearly as much as who we become as a result of our suffering.** My afflictions challenged my belief systems, and many of my ideologies evolved as a result.

I didn't fall on hard times solely because of an abusive relationship. There were other preexisting pieces to the puzzle. I made many destructive choices before, during, and after the years of abuse. It was a lifetime of abiding by toxic male ideologies that brought me to the brink. The abuse simply acted as a catalyst, causing me to dig deeper into those acidic beliefs. It solidified my toxic perspectives and negative behaviors until I could no longer function in everyday life. I was a mess. Only after the loss of my mother was I forced to reflect and unlearn many of my belief systems. I took to building myself back up, piece by piece. Reflection was the key that unlocked the lessons I needed to learn, and it was what promoted me to grow.

The reflections that follow exist to directly challenge the toxic masculine ideologies that took me down to rock bottom and continue to destroy the lives of both men and women alike. Each reflection section also offers **constructive guiding principles** that encourage men to grow so that everyone may prosper. All of them are important, but as my mentor and great friend (whom you'll meet later) Gene Miller would say, "Put first things first."

"Help"

The first thing I had to learn, and arguably the most important, was how to ask for help. Asking for help is the most obvious indicator of weakness in the toxic male identity. After all I had been through with my mother and the loss of our relationship, I still shamed myself for seeking assistance. It's tragic to think about how much of men's humanity is removed, and how much harder we make it on ourselves when we take the lone ranger approach. I walked away from that mentality years ago, but the hesitation still lingers. It's difficult, but today I ask for help because I know it *works*.

It is truer now than it has ever been that men must be tough. This message has been passed from generation to generation for good reason. However, our interpretation of the message is what perpetuates pain and stifles growth. We believe that we must never show weakness or vulnerability. That belief causes us to think rage, aggression, and disgust are acceptable alternatives to sadness, confusion, and appreciation. In fact, we are encouraged to hide all other emotions in general. Many men can't even say the word "emotion" without feeling discomfort. Instead, we project disgust onto people who express emotion, especially women (more on that later).

This belief system directly prevents us from becoming the best we can be—which is completely reliant on our ability to connect with ourselves and our surroundings. Connection requires openness and vulnerability. Unfortunately, being tough and stoic are foundational elements of toxic masculinity. This is why asking for help is such a profound detour from being a man. It's also where the road out to a beautiful life begins.

The question then becomes, how do we know when we need help?

First, we *admit* it. If done properly, looking in the mirror helps us get there. It is what allows us to build self-awareness—the compass which guides us on the journey to become our truest selves. When we know ourselves, we know our strengths (and our weaknesses). With self-awareness in place, asking for help can become an objective process that avoids ego-based inhibitors and promotes growth.

I challenge the young men I mentor to think of themselves as a chain. If every chain is only as strong as its weakest link, there is no shame in acknowledging a weak link. Nor is there reason to hide it. *Denial* is counterproductive and allows the weakness to remain. Only through nonjudgmental acceptance can a man take necessary action to strengthen his chain. It may seem counterintuitive to those who believe in toxic male ideologies, but **the most effective way for men to build strength is by first admitting they are weak.** "Strength" in this case is different than the toxic male ideology that teaches strength through isolation. Instead, constructive masculinity promotes men to build strength through *connection*. A connection-based method provides far more intellectual, emotional, and spiritual support than a solitary approach, thereby drastically increasing our ability to overcome even the most dire of circumstances.

I can't say for sure, but looking back, I suspect that's why I called my buddy Mike and asked for help. I *knew* I was in trouble. There was no denying it. I had no place to live. No job. No money. No concept of time, life, or health. I never considered killing myself, but I constantly thought about hurting others. I was forced to admit that I was in a dark place and couldn't get out of the hole on my own. I needed help.

Fortunately, Mr. and Mrs. C took me in because their son Mike and I had built a great friendship over a decade. This included regular interactions within their home, which allowed us to get to know each other and form a mutual trust. But that's not always the case.

People have biases about how men operate, and those biases can get in the way of understanding and helping them. People may hold a man to their idea of masculinity even though it has nothing to do with his reality. Men have always accounted for, and continue to account for, the vast majority of dark marks in human history—in broad strokes, slavery, rape, murder, genocide, and war. Men have been responsible for heinous violence and oppression for a long time. Men are also groomed to be emotionally dismissive and cold, which leaves those around them feeling invalidated and unseen. Understandably, people have built up quite a bias toward men as a result.

Toxic male ideologies don't just exist in men. They live in women, all sexual orientations, and other gender identities as well. Whether they realize it or not, **most people have an idea of how men are supposed to act and hold men to destructive standards, while also hypocritically vilifying the behaviors required to meet those standards.** People may harbor these ideas because of how we indoctrinate toxic male identity early or because they have a lifetime of experiences dealing with a consistent set of negative male behaviors. These beliefs and biases aside, toxic masculinity is the source of problems that affect us all.

For men to unlearn toxic male ideologies that hurt *everyone*, they must learn to open themselves up. It's easier said than done, as many men have been hurt by those closest to them. However, *opening up* is something that we must learn how to do in order to **commit ourselves to growth.** Never does a growth process look the same, but **the most consistent driver of personal growth is the internal acceptance of external energies.** It's difficult, to be sure. But the more men that do it, the more other men will do it. Why? Because growth brings men to a better place than toxic masculinity. It's that simple.

Only by committing ourselves to growth are we

granted an opportunity to pursue something we all desire—**a beautiful life.**

"You Have My Attention"

2009–10

The University of Pennsylvania has multiple high-rise dormitories that overlook the campus and the Philadelphia skyline. They are stunning. My sophomore and junior year dorm sat just across the way from them. It was called W.E.B. Du Bois, named after a brilliant Black academic, writer, and social activist. Although historic and symbolic, the dorm itself was an outdated dump. It was brick and dank, with lights that flickered, painting the walls a slimy yellow color. The lights made humming noises in the hallways. All the chairs and study spaces were ugly and bleak. There was no central air. The structure acted more like a dungeon than what one would expect from an Ivy League dormitory where students are paying an arm and a leg in tuition fees.

My buddies and I remained there for two years because the staff and students in it were nice, and it was nestled centrally among the places we liked to eat, party, and study. The dorm layout was also a rarity on campus because it allowed for four students to have their own rooms with a shared common space and bathroom, all separated from other students on the floor. It was our own suite, and in spite of the possibility that it was arguably the most outdated dorm on campus, we enjoyed our time there.

I parked near Du Bois to take a look at the place before

14

I headed up to the high rise to meet with a woman I had been seeing. She was in her senior year and writing her thesis, and I had already graduated. It felt weird to be back on campus without any academic or athletic responsibilities hanging over my head. Approaching Du Bois threw me for a loop. We had so many great times in there, but in this moment, being close was dejecting.

I sat down on a bench just in front of Du Bois to sort myself out before I went up to the high rise. I felt like a failure. I was back on a campus where I should have done very well but instead was a textbook case of mediocrity and disappointment. I didn't apply myself like I could have. For various reasons, I didn't see the point and lost motivation. My grades were fine, and I played two DI sports. I just knew that I didn't take the meat off the bone here. I had lost my way and still hadn't found it after I graduated. Being back was a harsh reminder of how adrift I really was and continued to be.

More than any other vice in college, pursuing women was at the top. By the end of junior year, I was well traveled, and I had a reputation for it. Seeing the dorm reminded me of a conversation I had with my roommate and great friend Mark's girlfriend, Steph. She and I jostled each other for laughs every now and again, but overall, we shared a friendship based on mutual respect. She was incredibly intelligent, far smarter than me, and showed more self-discipline at UPENN than I did. Her intellect and work ethic were admirable, and her personality was easy to get along with.

One night in the dorm, she unexpectedly gave me an earful about the nature of my interactions with women. She rarely gave me a hard time about anything, and it caught me off guard.

"Is this what you want? It's obvious that you're not happy. You know you're not happy. I don't understand why you keep doing it. Aren't you better than this? What are you doing?"

My guy buddies freely took part in listening to and laughing about the stories that came from my sexual promiscuity. I experienced things that were incredibly hard to believe, and my buds didn't believe me entirely. Then the stories were confirmed later on from other sources, and that made it even more funny. It was great storytelling, and we all laughed our asses off at the ridiculous situations that I found myself in. Despite the fact that those laughs were self-deprecating and came at my expense, Steph wasn't amused and evidently had kept her opinion to herself the whole time. So, when she expressed her disapproval and challenged me so abruptly, it was exceedingly hurtful. I didn't like that I was transparent to anyone. Her comments shook me to the core.

My buddies thought I was happy, and I gave them every reason to believe that I was. Steph cut through the bullshit and called me out. I didn't bother putting up a fight or debating her. She was right. I wasn't happy with that lifestyle, and I knew that I wasn't. I actually despised it. I was so grateful that she challenged me. It showed that she cared and saw through my veil. Yet, despite wanting to, I didn't have the guts to talk to her more about it. Instead, I just toned down the pace for senior year. After I graduated, the speed dropped to a snail's pace. My appetite for a fast and loose lifestyle had fizzled out, but I remained a mess.

As I sat on the bench, it became clear that I shouldn't be on campus and shouldn't go to the high rise for a date with the woman I was seeing. I knew something was missing, but I couldn't figure it out, so I did it anyway. Walking into the high rise was a reminder of just how new the structure and all its amenities were in comparison to Du Bois. The chairs were modern, clean, and laid out purposefully. The lights and architecture were pleasing and mostly metal and glass. The lobby was open and transparent with students playing ping-pong, listening to music, hanging out, and studying together. It was an interpersonal and interactive environment.

I called her from the lobby, and she came down to sign me in with security. She greeted me with a huge, genuine smile and a big hug. She smelled ridiculously good and looked stunning. On paper, she had it all. She was intelligent, ambitious, beautiful, and family-oriented. She held my hand to the elevator. The closer we got to her room, the more I felt that I was doing something wrong. I shouldn't be there. I didn't want to say anything to her about it because I couldn't explain why. I didn't want to hurt her feelings. I had no idea what I was doing.

We walked into her apartment. She had everything laid out for us. There were appetizers and glasses for the bottle of wine that I had brought. We sat down with our drinks and ate appetizers while we watched the movie. We talked easily enough, but my stomach was in knots. After a while, I started to feel comfortable and felt my guard drop. I stopped asking myself so many questions, and my brain stopped firing at warp speed. Then I went right back to questioning myself, and the voice from my conscience was deafening. I kept going back and forth mentally about whether I should be there or not. Both sides made sense, and I couldn't commit either way. My energies were split.

By the time the movie ended, it was pretty late, and I

had work at six o'clock the next morning. I was mentally and emotionally exhausted and very ready to leave. She went to her bathroom, and I got up, cleaned the space, and started walking to the door to leave. Then she came out of the bathroom wearing a thin, see-through bathrobe. She was a lot to take in visually. While also an excellent student, she was a competitive cheerleader and worked out constantly. She was in incredible shape. We had been talking to each other exclusively for a while, but I was in such a poor headspace that I never considered the possibility that she would initiate sex. My conscience was telling me to politely decline, say goodbye, and go home. I had heard this voice in my head many times in the past, but I forced myself to override it. In spite of every part of me saying, "Don't," I stayed and went along with her request.

Things escalated quickly, and although my conscience was still active, other elements had been engaged. As two healthy and active young people, our bodies responded the way that they are designed to.

As we got further into the process, I got overrun by my conscience. I was genuinely sick to my stomach over what was happening. I kept repeating the same thing in my head over and over.

"What am I doing?"

I could sense things were deteriorating. I was falling apart quickly. All the things that had happened during college and the year-by-year escalation of family trauma had worn me down to the point that I was hanging on by a very thin thread. And in that moment, when I was doing what I thought I was compelled to do as a man, the thread snapped. It became a moment of disconnect. Although my body was on, my head was off. **I simply was not there.**

It was only then that I realized I hated myself, hated the "who" I had become.

I went still and she noticed immediately.

Neither of us moved. After what seemed like forever, she broke the silence. "I don't know what you want, but it isn't me."

I heard the anger in her voice, but it didn't register within me. I could hardly breathe. It was all crashing down.

"Don't talk to me again." With this, I moved to the floor. She stayed in the bed.

The linoleum floor was ice-cold on my skin. I was shivering and stared into the black with my heart in my throat. I felt nothing. It was late. I looked at her clock and counted the minutes until it was time to leave for work at a credit card company a long drive away in Delaware.

At 3:45 a.m., I stood up and got dressed as quietly as I could. My eyes had adjusted, and I could see her clearly in bed. She had her back to me. I put my hand on her shoulder.

I whispered, "I'm so sorry," and left.

The hallway was bright and empty. It was a long walk down the corridor and around the corner to the elevator. As I passed by the bulletin boards, I could hear the pinned papers moving behind me. I pressed the button and was surprised by how quickly the doors opened. I stepped into the elevator and pressed *lobby*. The sudden drop made my balance shift from one foot to the other while I watched the floor indicator change one by one. The doors opened and I walked out, down the ramp, through the security door, and out into the cold. It was freezing.

I walked to the car and could feel the wind pulling the smell of her away from me. I didn't put my hands in my pockets or hunch over. I stood open, hoping the breeze would relieve me of all reminders of her by the time I got to my car. It didn't. I couldn't get her off me.

My car was an old, beat-up Nissan Maxima. It belonged to my dad originally, and he gave it to me as a graduation gift. It had hundreds of thousands of miles on it. The seats were crooked and still held a faint scent of our late family dog Rudy. But it functioned, and even in that moment, I still felt grateful for his gift. I pressed the car remote key and saw the orange blinker lights flicker. I heard it unlock. I opened the driver side door, got in, and slammed it shut. The doors were heavy and thick. The air inside the car was dense, cold, and still. I put the key into the ignition and heard it crunch against the slots. I turned the ignition and the car radio blared. I turned it off. The air coming out of the vents was cold. I cranked up the heat. The steering wheel was frozen and so was the shift. I put the car into drive, turned on my blinker even though no one was on the road, pulled out, and drove off campus.

That part of Philly is a ghost town early in the morning, but it still took me a while to get out of the city. The air didn't heat up until I was on the highway. I had a sixty-minute drive south to Delaware where I worked as a program director and facility manager at a mid-sized credit card company. My shift started at 6:00 a.m., and I had to get there by 5:45 a.m.

The only things I saw were the highway's painted dashes and the occasional reflector on the barrier separating both directions. It was pitch black. I was driving into nothing.

My mouth seemed welded shut. Each breath was small

and weak. The vibration on the wheel streamed through my hands to my arms and up to my shoulders. I knew the route by heart, but this time I felt lost.

I didn't know who I was or what I was doing. I didn't know why I was going to work. I didn't know whose body I was in. I couldn't sort my thoughts. Nothing made sense. And so, for the first time in my life, I submitted. My lips parted and my lungs opened. I took a deep breath and spoke upward to something I didn't know.

"Okay God. You have my attention."

Sex and Intimacy

It seems an odd thing to write about the drawbacks of sex for men. If nothing else, a "man" must be prepared and willing to perform sexually at all times because sexual performance is widely seen as a hallmark criterion of manhood. Societal expectations essentially demand that men be in control of their sexuality at all times, but also disregard any objections within their conscience to sex overall, lest they be subject to social shaming. I got swept up in those expectations. Despite having horrible past experiences and feeling many objections in that moment, I refused to change my behavior because of the belief systems that were drilled into my brain. "It doesn't matter if I don't want to. *This* is what men do."

As men, we are not adequately mentally groomed to see partners as people, as unique individuals with their own history, personal failures, issues, thoughts, emotions, and value. We aren't taught to see the person. Instead, we are taught to actively seek characteristics that are deemed desirable and affirm our manhood. Initially, the desirables are centered on face and body visuals. Then social status can creep onto the must-have list. Then other items jump on as well, and they can range from money, family background, and intelligence to agreeability and compliance. At its worst, toxic masculinity demands that men be in total control of their partner. The pursuit of agreeability and compliance disregards the partner's inherent individual value, and instead says more about the power and control the man seeks over his partner in order to feel like he's a *man*.

If we can take a step back from that, we may see that those items are distinctly inhumane. They are impersonal to the point that they can be considered commodities. Commodities are essentially products with assigned values. These values can be traded and upgraded: Hair can be longer. Breasts can be bigger. Personalities can be more submissive, etc. Just plug in any toxic male desire and it can be commodified.

While I would never tell any man that they shouldn't desire what they desire, I would challenge all men to consider other aspects that cannot be assigned a value and traded/upgraded in the *sex marketplace*. In fact, I'd challenge all men to depreciate the sex marketplace altogether.

The reason being: the sex marketplace is an extremely destructive mindset built upon hollow ideologies. It's *not* real. It speaks more to the way society views women than the reality of the situation. The truth is that every woman has inherent value. There is a marketplace for objects, but women are *not* objects. Therefore, the sex marketplace doesn't exist, and we cannot continue to treat women as if it does.

Sexual objectification has been a long-standing, unfounded injustice to women. From movies and magazines to social media platforms and fashion, nearly every society-based structure has objectified women somehow. It's interesting to note that while men have not been objectified in the same way as women, **men's sexuality has still been oversimplified.**

Men are not *exclusively* sexual beings. We are emotional, thoughtful, spiritual, and sensual beings as well. Whether we are aware of it or not, all components of our identity are included in our sexual experiences. We may think we can or should separate other components of ourselves from sex, but we can't. All aspects of men operate interdependently of each other whether we like it or not. However, societal messaging is so strong that it hypersexualizes men subconsciously, leaving many unaware that other components of their identity require attention (often the *most* attention) for personal growth, health, and connection with others.

The hypersexualization of men and the expectation to perform sexually at all times has muddied the waters in terms of personal choice as well. Many men assume that experiencing an erection means that they are sexually aroused and that they *must* act accordingly, while also disregarding any objections within their conscience. Although having an erection and sexual arousal are sometimes linked, it is not always the case. Erections often occur without arousal, and vice versa.

Nevertheless, society makes it seem like men must have intercourse when they have a genital response (aroused, consensual or not). There is no room for consideration or doubt, lest you become *less* of a man. It's a sad example of how **we've conditioned men not only to disregard their humanity, but to be completely unaware of it, and to reduce the complexities of their** masculine sexuality to arousal and genital response exclusively.

The reason I broke myself free from this false ideology was because it became glaringly apparent that I was losing myself to it. It wasn't true to who I really was, and my misaligned actions were hollowing me out. I may have been sexually promiscuous, but I was also the guy that people called to make sure a woman got home safely from the bar. It was far more important to me to be trusted with someone's safety. Deep down, I was more. I was someone else.

However, my hopeless dedication to toxic masculinity's standards of sexuality had severely wounded who I really was. By the time I was in that situation in the high rise, I could no longer continue to sexually engage with a woman without a genuine human connection. Even though we were a perfect match on paper, I felt nothing for her. Like sexual promiscuity, the relationship itself was hollow, but I still felt that I had to meet expectations. The compulsion to meet toxic masculine standards had taken me outside of myself and had grafted toxic beliefs with basic human sexual impulses.

Looking through this lens, sex without connection becomes a means to satisfy impulse. Over time, the appetite to satisfy impulse grows and grows. Impulses are, in and of themselves, reactive and temporary states of the human experience. While fulfillment of impulse can be enjoyable and satisfying, it comes at a cost.

Far more important than satisfying impulse is connection. The fact is that men are hardwired for connection. It is 100 percent necessary for our health and happiness. Engaging in sexual promiscuity by holstering a mindset centered on objectification severs our ability to connect.

Despite what traditional male messaging tells us, we are not meant to disconnect. Sex alone does not lend itself to fulfillment, happiness, or contentment. Sex alone hurts us and those around us.

Throughout my journey's engaging impulses, that truth grew and grew. As Steph said, "You aren't happy. Is this what you want?" I had no clue what I wanted. **When we don't know what we want, we just want** *more*. There were so many times when I wanted to stop but chose to continue. I was terrified of being judged and was disinterested or unaware of any alternative way a man was supposed to act. If we lose awareness of and do not embrace the truth—that men are sustained through connection and not sexual impulse alone—we will turn to harmful "defaults." These defaults are just ingrained habits built on harmful messaging about who men are supposed to be.

Toxic masculinity says that all sex is good for a man, but that's not true.

The truth was underneath my nose the whole time. I finally admitted that I needed genuine connection to meet my needs. In my case as a heterosexual, **I craved intimacy with one woman, and one woman only.**

Intimacy is a dirty word that is invasive and dangerous to traditional toxic male values. Like many men, the moment I felt close to a woman I would break it off—too threatening. However, building a positive, intimate, and monogamous relationship over a long period of time is so important for men to experience. Even just one good, committed, exclusive partner will do the trick. It will change a man for the better. It's not something to run from.

The playboy lifestyle is meaningless, while build-

ing an intimate relationship with one woman can promote personal growth. With that said, the man must hold himself accountable to his own happiness. It's not his partner's responsibility.

The same idea still applies to men with other orientations. There is enjoyment in sexual promiscuity, but the good stuff—the lasting value—is in the intimacy of a relationship. In this case, intimacy is not a euphemism for sex. It's a term used to describe the *closeness, safety, and connection* a man feels when in a meaningful, trustworthy relationship.

I'm not suggesting that men abstain from sex, nor that they engage in it. I'm simply offering a perspective that promotes the possibility that men consider the greater value in the mental, emotional, and spiritual energies associated with intimacy and connection, more so than simply satisfying physical impulse.

As men, if we focus ourselves to actively pursue connection with another person by valuing their intrinsic, unique value as a human being, we can finally free ourselves of the trappings of impulse.

It's more meaningful to suffer the joys and sorrows of intimacy than it is to continue abiding by toxic masculine sexual behaviors. By seeking genuine human connection, men can build intimacy, and only then can we be seen for our most natural, authentic selves. Being one's true self is a liberating state of being, to say the least. It is far better to be *a real person* who is intimate with *another real person* than to follow empty sexual practices that toxic male belief systems deem essential to manhood.

Self-Awareness and Purpose

I was dealing with many different identity-based concepts simultaneously. Sexual promiscuity was a prominent piece of my false toxic male identity for years, and realizing that I was not that person was the straw that broke the camel's back. If I wasn't that person, who was I? It made me question *everything* and kicked off an intense growth process.

At the time, I was managing a health and wellness program for a credit card company, and I was mostly left alone. After I'd finish my work duties, I'd dive into books. I stumbled on my first book while organizing the cabinets in the facility. It was a Bible hidden underneath some large manilla envelopes. I read it cover to cover. Then I read the Qur'an. Then I read books on Buddhism and Judaism. After reading through major religious texts, I could tell that exploring faith in God was going to take a lifetime, and I was okay with that. So, I redirected my focus to concentrate on learning about myself.

I read *The Alchemist, The Four Agreements, The Power of Now,* and multiple books by Thich Nhat Hanh. Within a three-month period, I had consumed well over forty books. I could not get enough. Finally realizing that I knew so little about life, I had so many questions that needed answers. I was learning a lot about myself, and I found that self-awareness to be empowering.

It was only when I began to challenge the toxic masculine ideologies I had followed for so long that I discovered I carried conflicting belief systems. It dawned on me that the pursuit of toxic masculinity was internally divisive. Meaning, **trying to be more of a "man" was making me less of myself.** There had been so many instances in my life when I could have chosen a smarter, more rewarding path that aligned to my true identity, but I didn't because "men don't do that."

The pressure to be a man is so strong and constant that oftentimes men don't even stop to question what they are doing. All that time and effort in pursuit of manhood leaves men miles away from their true selves, and eventually they break, like I did. That's when aimlessness sets in, and life can go dark pretty quickly because you don't know who you are or where you're going.

With self-awareness in place, trying to be a man gets demoted, and men can instead align their choices to their true identity as a unique human being. With the restrictions of toxic masculinity removed, life opens up to allow **beauty and purpose** to find their way in. Beauty and purpose are what make life worthwhile.

There are tons of books, podcasts, and sermons that describe the value of living a purposeful life in great detail. In Invictus (my mentoring business), we keep it simple and define purpose as a relentless dedication to something bigger than *you*. It is a concept that every single client is exposed to because it's just that important. It's why I mentor young men. It is my purpose in life.

However, as important as purpose in life can be, it is *not* required to live a good life. **You can still experience happiness and direction without purpose, if you are self-aware.** If you do not feel a burning passion to dedicate yourself to a greater cause, there is no need to beat yourself up. Do not allow the realization that you lack a defined purpose to create a void within you that doesn't need to exist.

Instead, live your life! Perform. Generate opportunity. Be adventurous. Love without limit. Be kind. Be generous.

Build meaningful relationships. That's still a winning formula. You can live a life of beauty without purpose.

In my mind, the difference between living a life of purpose and a life of beauty is not a difference in enjoyment, but in intensity. A life of purpose is a concentrated pursuit of beauty. A life of beauty is more of a generalized state of being.

Do not covet either experience as toxic masculinity would have us do by constantly comparing ourselves to others. Carrying toxic masculinity's innate condition of envy will commodify and contaminate the purity of beauty and purpose. By being envious, you will remove the uniqueness of each concept, thereby leeching the true value.

Purpose and beauty must be unique to you. Neither is meaningful if muddled with insincerity and a lack of authenticity. You'll miss the good stuff if you're blinded by your own insecurities or bogged down by your expectations based on what you perceive about other people's lives. Envy creates resentment.

Individualized beauty and purpose are *transcendental*, which means that they lift us out of all our broken human conditions (including envy).

Purpose will find you if it is meant to. In the meantime, there is no need to wait on purpose to be happy. Instead, unapologetically live well and be faithful to who you are.

Live a beautiful life that is true to *you*.

The Bay

2010–11

An Adventure Begins

Brian and I were teammates on the football team at UPENN and roommates for three years. We had become great friends and took road trips all over the place as often as we could. For this trip, we were driving south to Virginia with my dog, Rocco. I knew we were going to have a great time. We always did.

GPS said we were two hours away, but we knew it was closer to four hours.

Inevitably, we would hit this long stretch of highway riddled with traffic lights. To make it even more dull, the highway itself cut through cookie-cutter towns. The housing developments all looked the same, and the business campus layouts were identical. The worst part of the trip was this never-ending geographical block. We felt like we were on a hamster wheel seeing the same things over and over. It made time stand still.

Then all of a sudden, we broke free from purgatory and entered stunning rural farmland. The farms in Virginia's Chesapeake Bay area are all beautiful. Each is unique with blemishes and multigenerational character. The aroma is distinct. Smells of diesel, animals, vegetation, and salty ocean air all hitch a ride on the breeze that runs over the area's flat topography. The smell could only be experienced here, and it added nostalgia to our trip.

There was a large Hispanic population down here, and Brian was fluent in Spanish, which made things easier when we stopped to eat at the only restaurant within twenty miles of Brian's family home on the bay. It was a Mexican place, and I proudly ate my weight in tacos each visit.

From there, we came into the final stretch of the road trip, which was lined with large old trees, mostly pines, and sweeping farm fields that stretched into the horizon. There were no lights, and the street signs were difficult to see. Thankfully Brian had been here a thousand times and knew the way.

"Turn here," Brian said.

I flipped on my blinker and turned slowly. Even though I never recognized the street from the highway, I could tell you every detail once inside. I knew about the power lines and inlets. I knew it was exactly two miles until we reached his family's place. We drove those last two miles at a snail's pace with the windows down and radio off. We always made a point to soak in the vibe and leave our worries miles away from us back on the highway.

Brian reached into the cooler that we kept behind the center console, grabbed two beers, and cracked those suckers open. He gave one to me and said his patented toast.

"Cheers, brother."

"Cheers. Get some. Thanks for having me down here, Bri."

We sipped those ice-cold beauties and cruised. I never drove under the influence, much less drank while in the act of driving, so I held this tradition very close to my heart. There were no police out here. There was no need. People acted right, and despite feeling guilt from breaking the law in this one instance, being in this place brought out a levity in me.

We turned onto his family property, which sat right on the water. It was a humble two-story house with a small back deck and glassed-in porch that overlooked the bay. We parked next to the side door and downed the rest of our beers. Rocco started whimpering and yelping uncontrollably. He loved it here. Brian opened the back door, and Rocco leaped out and immediately started peeing on everything. Brian reached into the side compartment and pulled out a tennis ball.

"Hey, Roc! Roc! Go get it!"

Brian chucked the tennis ball over the dock that led out to the water, and Rocco sprinted full speed down the dock, leaped off of the edge, and disappeared. It always made us laugh to see the water splash. We never had to worry about him. He always stayed within sight.

Brian opened the trunk, which we had stuffed with our duffel bags and tons of groceries. We packed big so that we never had to leave to get anything.

"All right, Bri, one trip. Everything in. Test of manhood."

Despite having known Brian for years, it never ceased to amaze me how freakishly strong he was. He played defensive end for the football team and easily won strongest in the weight room. Our buddies and I used to joke with him about his mutant strength all the time.

"Think you can handle those groceries, Bri? Need a spotter?"

He played along and got into proper lifting form, took a big bracing breath, and lifted the groceries like he was lifting a car (which I had seen him do before). Then he casually curled them and put the key in the door as if the bags were filled with feathers. We both walked into the house, and it was exactly as I remembered it. There was a very small kitchen, a four-by-four island, two couches, a coffee table, a fireplace, and a small, outdated TV all underneath an open two-story ceiling. There were several bedrooms, each decorated minimally but with charm. Looking out of the kitchen toward the bay, you'd see into the glassed-in porch, which was decorated with things found in the area. There were seashells, driftwood, and a few other local trinkets. There were family photos everywhere of time spent on this property. Just being in the house drummed up feelings of good times spent with good people that I had never met.

Within thirty minutes of arrival, we were completely set up. The grill was hot, and we could hear the sound of meat sizzling. The smell made me drool, and I chased it down with cold beer while sitting on the deck.

The view was stunning. The bay just went on and on. It looked more like the open ocean. Even though there were neighbors on either side, no one interfered with each other's vista. Everyone was respectful and stayed out of each other's business. The code of conduct was written in the air waves.

It was an escape from the modern world.

The following morning, we slammed coffee, water, and a mountain of oatmeal to prepare for our early morning workout, one of two for the day.

Brian was training to pursue excellence as a Marine, and I was training to enter the Army. We were both former Division I athletes and had borderline issues with our competitive nature. Training together was a blast, and we pushed each other past our limits over and over again. We were grateful to be there, and training to the point of collapse made us feel like we earned the downtime.

We finished up the morning's training and then cooked a massive breakfast of eggs, pancakes, and bacon. We hopped on the WaveRunners and went out into the bay to explore. He showed me every nook and cranny of the area and where we would go camping the following day. The idea sounded amazing, but it didn't look possible. I asked him where we would dock and how we would trek into the island, which had no clear entry.

"We'll come back when the tide is different, and you'll see it. Not too many know about it."

On the ride back to the house, he directed me to follow him. He was about three hundred yards away from me in the middle of the ocean. To my complete shock, he stepped off of his WaveRunner and started walking on water!

I drove over and saw that Brian was standing on a thin sand dune. It was one hundred yards long and shaped like an "S." I found a good spot to park, jumped off the WaveRunner, and started running up and down the dune, which was surrounded by miles of water. It was amazing!

"Bri! This is fucking crazy! How did you find out about this?"

"I literally stumbled on it."

I eventually sat down on the dune and looked out on the bay to soak in the experience. I was there for ten minutes, but it felt like hours. All I could hear was the ocean water lapping up against the dune. Brian was doing the same thing on another part of the dune a good stretch away from my spot.

We eventually headed back to the house, where we ate lunch and then worked out again—big time sprint session.

We were done training for the day. I was completely wrecked and didn't bother trying to hide how good I felt. A smile was tattooed across my face, and I wore it shamelessly while drinking up the sun on the deck with the grill's aroma filling my nose.

As we often did, Brian and I got a good buzz going that afternoon and into the night. A warm belly was the right status for each of us; neither of us liked to get drunk.

Brian fell asleep on the couch with Rocco snuggled underneath his legs. Both were snoring. I had to take a piss and went outside to not wake either of them. The night was so clear.

There was no wind. I didn't hear any waves. The bay water was like glass, and there wasn't a cloud to be seen or a man-made light anywhere. The moon was bright with stars blanketing the sky.

I sat down on a bench and was completely alone. In that moment, my goals didn't matter—neither did my education, sport, or career ambitions. I had no personal history, failures, or conflicts. My problems vanished.

It was just me, the ocean, and the night sky. I connected with my surroundings and with myself. My belly relaxed. My breathing became rhythmic and deep. I inhaled salty, fresh air through my nose.

Nothing mattered. I was still.

Jellyfish

We went through our same routine the following morning. Coffee, eat, workout, eat again, chill, and workout again. The second workout was a swim to the other side of the bay and back. Brian said it was about a sixty-minute swim, thirty minutes each way. I was a strong swimmer and the salty water provided buoyancy that pool water did not. I wasn't in love with the idea because no one knew where we would be and we had no way of asking for help if we got in trouble. Brian had two instant-inflatable devices, and we both tied one to our ankles with a few feet of length so it wouldn't interfere with our swimming gait. They were bright and easily visible. That was enough for me.

Out we went.

The water was warm in the shallow and chilled the more we swam out. My imagination started running wild with scenes of sharks and massive squid playing out in my head. These visions continued for a while, and then suddenly we were swimming in a massive jellyfish forest. It happened that fast. Hundreds upon hundreds of fist-sized jellyfish were everywhere. It was a real-deal situation.

Neither of us panicked. We backed up, remained calm, and swam around them. We finally reached the other side, turned right around, and swam all the way back without interruption. We hit a good rhythm and crushed the second half of the swim.

Within a comfortable distance from the dock, I put my feet down and walked the last fifty yards to shore. I whistled for Rocco. He came trotting over to me, made sure to get a good back scratch, and then walked to Brian, who was examining the motor on the small boat fastened to the dock. I looked around. It was insanely hot.

The grass was abrasive, spikey, and not at all soft. I still walked on it comfortably without sandals but noticed how differently it felt from the grass back up north. The heat made the vegetation harsh. The needled bushes were not kind to a passerby, and the bugs were ruthless once they got going. I loved looking for the spiders, though. They were the size of my palm and black with sharp green legs and a yellow-checkered ass. I could see their eyes and fangs without having to squint. They were menacing, and I loved feeding them sluggish flies and cicadas.

"Yo, Bri!"

"Sup?"

"The jellyfish . . ."

"Shit man, are you kidding me with that? Never seen that many."

"Let's go ahead and file that one away in the *never fucking do that again* folder."

"Happily."

I felt good that we handled ourselves well given an unexpected change in circumstances that could have ended very poorly had we panicked, but guilty that we put ourselves in that position at all. Stupid.

We spent the afternoon prepping for the evening. We were going camping out on that island. I had no idea what to expect, but I was looking forward to it.

Private Island

Later that evening, just as the sun was setting, we loaded up the small, beat-up old boat with a cooler filled with beer, trash bags, and food. We turned the lights on in the house and put a marker at the end of the dock. I assumed this was done for visibility purposes, in case we came back when it was dark. With lifejackets on, Brian, Rocco, and I got in the boat and shoved off.

Rocco had his hind legs on the boat and his front propped up on a seat. He pointed his nose and sniffed while looking forward. I sat closely behind him to make sure he didn't go overboard. Brian was driving, and we cruised toward the horizon and listened to the sound of the water washing alongside us. It was a long trip, but we weren't in a hurry and enjoyed the journey.

Brian veered and brought us in toward the island. As we got closer, I could see exactly what he was talking about earlier in regards to the access point. The tide changed the landscape considerably, and we would have to haul the boat up by hand. Brian and I jumped off the boat and into the sand. Rocco did the same. We lifted the boat up, brought it ashore, and fastened it to a tree. We climbed up a steep fifteen-foot bank and walked into the tree line about twenty yards and then started looping back to the shore side. We set to work building a small fire in a cleared sandy space surrounded by logs. The smoke smelled good and kept the bugs at bay.

We sat down on the logs and looked out over the bay. The sunset was in full swing. It looked like a watercolor painting. All the pinks, purples, oranges, and reds embraced each other over Atlantic Ocean blue. The colors were brilliant. It looked like the water was on fire when it rippled. I had never seen anything like it.

"What a view," I said.

"Never gets old," Brian responded.

With that, we cracked open a six-pack and sat with our backs to the fire and looked out over the bay. We talked freely over the first beer, but after we opened a second, neither of us said a word.

When there was a little sunlight left, we cleared the camp of any sign of us being there. We threw wet sand on the fire to fully put it out. Then we climbed down the bank, freed the boat, and headed back.

All was silent.

Brotherhood

If I could wish any one thing for young men, it would be that they receive the stabilizing energy that brotherhood with other men provides. It is a connection that cannot be replicated, and beautiful moments can unfold that stay with you for the rest of your life as a result.

I consider myself beyond blessed in this way. I am fortunate to have built a lasting brotherhood with a small handful of men: Brian, PJ, Doc, Buz, Mike, and Dave. These bonds have stood the test of time, all lasting for decades. I have shared adventures with each of them, all of which are as dear to me as the trips down to the bay with Brian. Those adventures and relationships have shaped who I am.

Building these relationships requires many things that most young men are unfortunately not willing to give. It requires time, effort, and patience, which in some cases may include bumps, bruises, and a few arguments along the way. There is a depth to these relationships that cannot be experienced without mutual vulnerability.

Even still today, writing those words creates a sense of discomfort in me due to the residual effects left from traditional masculine ideologies, which very clearly state that vulnerability is weakness. I remind myself that the vulnerability expressed amongst these friendships is done on our terms. We connect in our own way, which may seem odd to some but is normal for us. I freely admit my bias toward our process in achieving a connection wherein we can freely express love toward each other without feeling emasculated.

It is noticeable. When we brought our girlfriends, who eventually became our wives, to hang out with us, they were quick to comment about how different it was to hang around a bunch of testosterone-ridden water buffalo who challenged each other yet somehow managed to be kind as well. It creates an environment where everyone can let their guard down and be themselves. We have built an amazing crew over the years, and the trust shared among my buddies has extended to their significant others. Our *family* has grown considerably, and with that growth comes a sense of belonging that contributes significantly to overall health and happiness.

That's the power of brotherhood. It creates a gravity that firmly plants all feet on the ground. With a stabilizing force like that in life, roots will run deep. One can weather storms by leaning on one another and share good vibes when times are bright.

I genuinely don't know what I'd do or who I would be without these relationships. What I can say confidently is that I would not be where I am today. I would not have gotten through the dark days without my friends being who they are. Just the thought of them was enough to prevent me from crossing lines in tempting moments.

For men, brotherhood is not simply friendship. In many ways, it is *more*. Brotherhood is a bond that strengthens its participants and removes the trash. This level of honesty may not necessarily be found even in the best of friendships. Within brotherhood, there is no room for falsity or fluff. Those characteristics are pushed out by an unspoken code of conduct that leaves no space for artificiality or selfish behavior. Instead, honesty occupies that space, and with that comes standards of behavior. Everyone is silently held accountable to being a "good dude." As we mature, the bar is held to being a "good man."

You may choose selfish decisions at the expense of your

friends every once in a while, but that can never happen within your brotherhood. You may want your friends to lie to you and tell you what you did is okay, but a brother will hit you square between the eyes and tell it to you straight.

A friendship will protect your feelings.

A brotherhood will protect your *character*.

As time and life allows, I encourage all young men to put the time in, make the sacrifices, and open their hearts to the idea of building brotherhood with other men. You will be a much stronger, more resilient, and more compassionate individual because of those relationships. The payoff is immense and everlasting in all areas of your life.

I have nothing but love for my friends. The brotherhood we built has pulled me through unimaginable dark places, and for that, I am grateful.

2012

"Hold on a Minute, Babe"

I must have done something right in my training with Brian, because I found myself in the Army. It was 3:30 a.m. and I dragged my ass out of the top bunk and climbed down as quietly as I could to not wake my bunkmate. Cox was snoring a few rows down. We were many weeks into Army Basic Combat Training, and I still couldn't understand how he got anything done with how he waited until the last minute. Regardless, the dude was a high achiever with great presence.

Cox was a Black, cerebral scholarship football player standing at six foot four, 255 pounds, and an expert code writer. We could not get along any better as we shared a twisted sense of humor, and it is impossible not to like him. We had each other's backs and shared a like-minded philosophy. We were ruthlessly dedicated to making sure the guys around us excelled and were the first to volunteer for missions. We were lucky to sleep or get opportunities to eat. The trade-off was that the drill sergeants pretty much left us alone and would sometimes include us in private briefings in their office which was a closed, walled space within our barracks. Being granted privacy and information was invaluable in a place where everyone was treated the same.

The Army is an interesting world in this way. I was shocked by how one barrack could house over fifty completely different men. The diversity was impressive in itself, but the paths that led each of us to take the oath were even more interesting. No two stories were alike, and I enjoyed learning about each of them. I also admired how the Army could be consistently successful in taking a melting pot of individuals and turning them into a single, functioning unit despite personal differences. The camaraderie was unlike anything that I had experienced.

We were constantly being forced into each other's personal space. We had to sleep, shit, bathe, eat, and sweat literally on top of each other. The forced personal proximity was rarely taken personally or perceived as a sexual advance. It was the opposite really. We would wrestle, fight, and show physical affection and emotion freely. Personal differences and background didn't matter. If you worked your ass off, took orders, and were a team player, you were embraced by your fellow soldiers. Period.

The shadow side to that code could be cruel. If you didn't abide and took your defiance to an extreme, you could be socially isolated, hazed, or even beaten. Laziness, stubbornness, and selfishness were punished severely in one way or another. Regardless of negative attitudes, Cox was adamant that everyone be motivated and supported to graduate basic training, and I admired his dedication to the platoon.

However, at times Cox and I would disagree in how to achieve that goal. He sometimes employed an approach that I did not agree with because it included breaking the rules. But I could not argue with the results he produced and therefore willingly turned my back on many of his infractions which were almost entirely harmless. Some were pretty damn funny actually. Weeks earlier, I had gone into the utility closet to get bleach to clean the latrines. Instead of seeing the usual brooms, buckets, and mops, I instead found Cox jerking off while talking on his cell phone to his girlfriend. He turned around, saw me, and said, "Hold on a minute, babe."

Instead of stopping and covering himself, he kept going. Being in the barracks with over fifty young men, I saw many acts of ridiculous penis jokes, contortions, and abstractions. We were all calloused to each other's genitalia and sexual expressions, so finding Cox in this position was not sensational. **I was far more impressed at his ability to hide a cell phone.** We all had turned in our cell phones months ago. I was amazed that he hid it successfully despite the many unexpected comprehensive searches conducted by drill sergeants to apprehend contraband. When I saw him beating his meat, all I said was, "Make it quick. We gotta go."

Affection, Emotion, and Hypermasculinity

In some hypermasculine atmospheres—where themes like toughness, order, effort, and violence are a way of life—it's not uncommon to see men form relationships wherein they can be affectionate and emotional toward each other, even if those behaviors are deemed unacceptable outside of those environments. My Army buddies (like Cox) and I often shared emotions about our loved ones and beat the hell out of each other every chance we got, all done as expressions of camaraderie and trust, which were otherwise unattainable outside of the demands of the Army. I believe this is a small example of a larger phenomenon amongst men due in large part to a subconscious collective approval of each other's masculinity, which allows men to express themselves, or at least more of themselves, when they know that the other men meet the same standards of masculinity as they do. *Some* men can thrive in these microclimates, but a strict, standardized code of behavior is not a cost that all men are willing or even capable of paying. Nor should they.

How a man expresses emotion and shows affection is up to him, but emotion and affection need to be accessible and accepted throughout the masculine experience, not just exclusively in hypermasculine environments. I celebrate hypermasculine environments if they are inclusive, compassionate, and inspirational because those ideologies consistently help men find their best selves. "Best self" in this case does rely on the ability to build relationships where men can express emotion and be affectionate, especially toward other men. Interpersonal emotion and affection are vital components of health and need to be included as acceptable masculine behaviors if we are to promote personal growth and collective brotherhood amongst men.

"Again"

Today, we were going to leave the barracks to conduct field missions. Cox and I received our orders from the drill sergeants and relayed them to the platoon. We spent the next hour getting everyone ready. Then, we were both called back to the drill sergeants' office. They sat us down for a gear inspection.

Cox and I both made sure that neither of our rucksacks exceeded the forty-pound limit for basic combat training and made sure the weights for the rest of the platoon were up to standards. Our drill sergeants weighed our rucks and they both came in just under forty.

"Double them."

I could have sworn that Cox started drooling. He was a challenge junkie. I too was excited about the challenge and was curious if we could effectively move with eighty pounds on our backs.

Off we went into the field. For today, the field meant a forest as opposed to other days when it could mean a firing range or obstacle course. The woods of Fort Benning are beautiful and bizarre. They are completely untouched, but there are trails and divots made by soldiers from the past throughout the area. There is also a faint smell of gunpowder everywhere. The animals are plentiful and most of them are not friendly. When we went out into the woods, it felt like we were in the middle of nowhere and completely cut off from civilization.

We did our normal drills and operations. It was nothing new and I was disappointed. I had gotten pretty fired up for *something*. We were eventually asked to get into formation, which I assumed was to take us back to our pickup point. Instead, we started marching away from our pickup point. That's when I knew something was up. We eventually stopped at an open field just in front of a dense forest. We were then divvied up by platoon and brought side to side.

Our orders were simple. We were going to execute sniper evasion maneuvers while going through the forest. The first soldier to make it through the forest gained points for his platoon, and the first platoon in its entirety to finish gained even more points. Sniper evasion meant starting with your chest and face down in the dirt, then popping up, taking two small, quick steps, and falling back to the dirt as quickly as possible. "I'm up, he sees me, I'm down" was the cadence, and you could cover three yards at most with each repetition. In the past, we did this drill with our weapons in-hand and without our rucks. It is completely exhausting at the fifty-yard mark. This time, we were ordered to do it with our weapons and rucks through a quarter mile of forest! Cox and I had eighty pounds on our backs, and we each weighed roughly 230 pounds by that point. Each "up" meant that we would be pushing over 300 pounds off the ground.

Cox looked at me with his eyes open wide and a devilish smile stretched across his face. I looked back at him and blew a snot rocket in his direction and mouthed a silent "Fuck you, Cox." We couldn't see where the finish line was, but we didn't care. The race was on between us. We competed every chance we got, and with victory came bragging rights.

"*Move!*"

And we started. Cox was much stronger than me, but I had more stamina. I thought I may have to pace myself, but if I misjudged the distance, then he would beat me. If I judged correctly, then I would beat him. But there was no way of knowing, so we both went full tilt right away. At first, he had me by a couple steps but then I started to creep up. After about fifty yards, I had a ten-yard lead on him and he was getting tired. Then after one hundred yards, I had a twenty-yard lead on him and could barely make him out behind me. I put my head down and just went to work. There was no end in sight, and I was completely wrecked. It was a hot day and I had sweat pouring out of my helmet down my nose. Each "up" for me looked more like a cobra arching its back. I couldn't do any more push-ups. I had to prop myself up one limb at a time. Each "I'm down" was a flop. I couldn't control the fall. My uniform had ripped open, and my knees and elbows were bleeding everywhere. The pressure in my face was building and eventually became incredibly painful. I couldn't see anyone around me, which was never a good thing. We were never allowed to be alone. We always had to have a "battle buddy" near us.

I called out, "*Cox!* Where you at, man?!"

I could barely hear him respond far behind me and off to the side.

"*Cox!* Anyone near you?"

"*No!*"

"I'm up to your left. Let's link up in the middle."

We met up in the middle and continued forward. It wasn't about the race now. No one was near us. We had no idea how much farther we had to go. We focused solely on finishing our mission. We did our best to lock in a pace together, which was like a snail's crawl, but we didn't have anything left in the tank. It was as fast as we could go. We were both covered in sand, dirt, and blood.

Eventually, we saw a clearing. Cox had puked on himself, and I was dry heaving repeatedly. Just ahead, we caught a visual of him. It was our Drill Sergeant Valenta. At roughly six feet tall, he always stood perfectly upright, and the brim of his hat covered his piercing blue bombardier eyes. He was one of very few drill sergeants that didn't yell often. He spoke clearly with unquestionable authority. He was an Airborne Ranger with multiple tours under his belt in two different wars. His standards were superhuman. He expected nothing less than our best and enforced those expectations fairly and swiftly. I had never met anyone like him, and I greatly admired his leadership and training philosophies. I never wanted to let him down, and neither did Cox.

Cox and I could clearly see that we were going to finish first with no one even remotely close to us. No one was even visible. Drill Sergeant Valenta stood at the finish line which was only five yards away from us. We had two more up downs ahead of us. We completed one, and just as we were peeling ourselves off the dirt and about to finish our last repetition, Drill Sergeant Valenta spoke.

"Freeze."

We staggered to the position of attention with sand, snot, and blood covering our faces. We could barely stand upright and were swaying on our feet just one step away from the finish line. Drill Sergeant Valenta extended his right arm with his knife-edged hand pointing behind us.

"Again."

We returned to the starting point and did it again. We finished dead last.

Strength of Spirit

I will never forget that drill for the rest of my life. It took me way past my limits and into a state of physical, mental, and emotional exhaustion that I didn't think was possible. That was just on the first go around. The second was far, far worse. Cox and I barely had the strength to breathe, let alone do up downs through that forest again. I had blown out all the blood vessels in my face, and the veins in my eyes had popped from the strain. Cox had tears streaming down his face and so did I, but it wasn't because we were emotional. Our bodies were panicking and expressed tears without our permission. We never spoke about it again and neither did anyone else in our platoon or the other platoons. I didn't see any of them, but I did see a handful of drill sergeants. They stood and watched Cox and I with their chins up and chests out as we finally collapsed over the finish line.

Whenever I think back at that moment, emotions flood the gates. Despite the controlled environment and the fact that it was only a drill, it took me to a deep place within myself. That place can withstand damn near anything. I have gone to that bunker many times over the course of my life since that moment. Those moments weren't controlled or sterile. They certainly weren't drills. They were the real deal and I only got through them because I was willing to dig deep into that space and push through. I am forever grateful for being pushed to that point and meeting my soul.

I believe that we are all born with an untouchable area within our spirit that can only be accessed when life is painful and times are hard. It's something that all men need to know they have, even if they never have to use it. The knowledge that it exists is powerful. It doesn't remove fear or pain. It removes the possibility that you may quit because of the fear and the pain.

A truly resilient man still experiences pain like a weak man does. The difference is that a resilient man knows how to *trudge*. A trudge is a heavy walk through difficult, harsh conditions. It requires an indomitable will and willingness to sacrifice parts of yourself to get where you need to go.

The sacrifice of self is what I believe men are not willing to do. They don't want to say goodbye to their sense of comfort and their ego. However, storms will drown our ego. Being brought low introduces us to the weakest parts of ourselves. **When we are at our weakest, we encounter our greatest strength—our spirit.**

Spiritual strength is not human. It is not of this earth. It transcends our bodies and provides us with tremendous power mentally, emotionally, and physically. Spiritual strength can weather any storm and withstand the pain therein.

Should you get all the way to the finish line and be sent back to the start, do it again. If nothing else, do it out of spite. Do not allow circumstances to make you into someone that you are not. Do not become a liar and betray yourself. Do not be a quitter. Do not join the timid souls on the sidelines who "neither know victory nor defeat." Remain in the fight. Dig deep. Knuckle up. Push through.

Finish.

Five against Fifty

We were three weeks away from graduation. I had been platoon leader for a month straight, which was the longest anyone had held the position in our platoon. We were far and away ranked number one in all categories and the clear favorites for Platoon of the Cycle. I was in contention for Soldier of the Cycle with three other soldiers, one from second, third, and fourth platoon respectively.

We were gearing up for our longest stretch out in the field. By this time, one of our two drill sergeants had been replaced with a new one, Drill Sergeant Valencia, a six foot three jacked Puerto Rican covered in tattoos. Unlike Drill Sergeant Valenta, Drill Sergeant Valencia was loud and in your face. He was a former Marine with tons of battle experience and had been selected as Drill Sergeant of the Cycle multiple times. The men in the platoon were terrified of him to the point that they asked me to stand beside them when they asked him for clarifications on orders and tasks. I felt no fear toward him. I admired him. He had a monstrous physical presence, and Cox and I respectfully challenged him in this way every chance we got. His physical training was more structured but equally as difficult as Drill Sergeant Valenta's approach. Drill Sergeant Valenta elevated us in every category, and Drill Sergeant Valencia was the one who took the platoon to number one in the standardized physical fitness tests. He knew Cox and I liked to nip at his heels, and he brutalized us. It was great.

We got out into the field and started doing multiple missions. It was easily the most fun we had during the entire training cycle. Drill Sergeant Valencia chose five of us from first platoon for a secret night mission. It was me, Cox, Alvarez, Barnett, and Daley. All of us were solid, liked each other, and made a great team. We were ordered to sneak into third platoon's camp undetected, neutralize them, and stake claim to their center space. The five of us stripped down to the bare minimum. We wore our uniforms and carried our weapons. That was it. Off we went into the forest over a mile away. We had no drill sergeants watching us.

Third platoon had an excellent position. Their camp sat on top of a hill, and the only access points were from a road or from the base of the hill. They were well situated and had a ton of talent. However, they had no discipline and that's what we decided to exploit.

At dusk, we split up into groups of two and three and held our positions until it was dark. Third platoon built their formation on the perimeter with a cluster of multiple groups of soldiers. Being undisciplined, they started whispering and using their flashlights, which told us exactly where they were.

We each had two dummy grenades, and all our watches were synchronized. I remembered from our grenade training day that you should typically refrain from throwing a grenade uphill because it could roll back down and blow your ass up. So, Daley and I crawled over the course of an hour in the forest undetected to a higher position. We were less than thirty yards away from the side of their camp. Cox, Alvarez, and Barnett lay quietly, perpendicular to us just off the side of the road. Our watches were synchronized, and we waited for our predetermined time to attack their camp.

It was time. I stood up silently, pulled the pin, and hurled that sucker at one of their tents. It landed just short and rolled in between two of their tents. It made that familiar hissing sound. I could hear a few guys saying, "What the fuck is that?" and then *boom*. Daley had thrown his grenade one second behind mine. *Boom*. With two grenades, we took out three of their tents, "killing" twelve soldiers. Their entire platoon turned and looked to the tents instead of securing their perimeter. Afterward, Cox told me that he, Alvarez, and Barnett jogged over fifty yards and casually threw all of their grenades into the camp, obliterating the entire front line because no one looked to the perimeter. All of this happened within a few seconds. Then we opened fire and had them pinned in a cross fire. In less than thirty seconds, the five of us had neutralized their entire camp of fifty soldiers. They still had no idea where we were. They started turning on their flashlights, and by that time, we had sprinted into the center of their camp and were sitting on their equipment boxes, watching them try to find us. It was hysterical. They eventually made us out and conceded that they had been absolutely destroyed. Even their drill sergeants admitted defeat. I started talking to their platoon commander to discuss the terms of surrender and saw Cox in the corner of my eye. He was talking to the other leaders in third platoon and walking them through what we did—a team player all the way. The soldiers on the perimeter showed a catastrophic lack of discipline and didn't follow the basic instruction that we all had received up until that point. All five members of our team talked a little smack but mainly coached up third platoon's leaders so they wouldn't make the same mistakes.

We ran back to our camp along the road because it was dark and we didn't want to risk any chance of getting lost in the woods. When we returned, Drill Sergeant Valencia was nowhere to be found. We weren't drilled that night and just ran our normal security operations. We knew we had done well because Drill Sergeant Valencia left us alone.

The following night was one of the most memorable of my life. The entire cadre of drill sergeants put together a siege on all four of our platoons. Each platoon had set up camp along the ridges of a giant gully and each had a side. There were two hundred soldiers all in one area, and that area should have been easily defensible. Dressed in all black, the drill sergeants snuck in undetected and threw dummy grenades at each of the platoons. Every platoon froze except for ours. Cox barked orders to our men on the ridge to face outward and secure the perimeter. I ordered the men on the inside to use their flashlights and point them inward to catch the intruders. I knew that grenades could only be thrown so far, and based off the explosions, I had correctly made the assumption that the drill sergeants were in the camp somewhere and not outside of the perimeter.

We did catch them.

The first sergeant and captain both personally congratulated first platoon for our discipline and even took me aside privately to congratulate me on my quick thinking, clear, decisive orders, and cool, calm, and collected leadership while under attack. They also made sure to correct me on several things and offered me ways to improve. Their voices were stern. I had missed some things that would have prevented a loss of life during a real invasion. I felt a bittersweet combination of pride and humility.

As part of the terms for exchange of our hostages, we were promised to be left alone for the night provided we did not break our military bearing and followed previous orders.

Two hundred soldiers were left alone in total silence under a cloudless night sky.

Nobody made a sound.

Silence

Of the two hundred soldiers, only 15 percent at most were college graduates. The vast majority were recent high school graduates from all parts of the country with all races, religions, and orientations represented. There was conflict, but overall, we got along well. As you can imagine, when you consider the nature of a large group of young men like that, unless the drill sergeants were around, they never shut the hell up. Dozens of men were yapping or whispering at all times.

That night after the drill sergeants lit us up and we held our ground, no one made a sound, not one single person. The collective sense of accomplishment was profound. We all came together to complete our mission as a single operating unit, and the feelings from that success were too good to ruin. It unified us, and for one night, everyone was quiet.

After my final briefing, I lay down in my sleeping bag in the hole that I had dug earlier. I looked up at the sky. We were far away from any city, in the middle of the woods. There was no light pollution. The night sky looked like a bad CGI movie. There were tens of thousands of stars. I could see planets. There were shooting stars all night long. I didn't think about anything. I let myself sink into the moment.

Men must have those moments. All must be silent. We need to feel small and be engrossed in a sense of wonder. We must seek humility and realize that we are not at the center of the universe. We must allow ourselves to fully connect to our surroundings and to the moment. Realistically, it takes a lot to bring men to that point. Some never get there. Our egos are too great, and our inner voices run too hot. We have to make a focused effort to humble our ego and silence our thoughts in order to be quiet and still. That kind of mental discipline is an important skill to have.

When our waters are calm, only then can we see down to the bottom. Seeing into the depths of our spirit, we can sometimes experience profound personal realizations.

For me, in that moment under the stars, I accepted that my life didn't matter, and my eventual death would be inconsequential to the masses. It was liberating. I only *mattered* to the people close to me. I felt a profound sense of gratitude for those people and took a silent vow to never again refrain from telling someone how I feel about them. I continue to uphold that promise by expressing myself to the people I love every day.

The Race

The following morning, we were ordered to suit up, mount up, and move out. Drill Sergeant Valencia took us all into a hilly part of the woods and informed us we would be doing a formation run. Generally, formation runs were conducted in physical training gear, which was shorts and a T-shirt with sneakers. Today we were going to go for a run wearing full battle gear with our rucks and weapons. Drill Sergeant Valencia was an athletic freak, known for his superhuman performance. I had been dying for an opportunity to race him.

I stood next to Drill Sergeant Valencia, and the platoon was formed to our side. He whispered orders to me, and I shouted them out to the platoon. Off we went.

It started as a light jog. Running in formation was one of my favorite things. You really felt like a team, a functional unit. Then he gradually increased the pace. Despite the rugged terrain, we kept up. Then he relayed an order that we could break formation to accommodate the terrain, but we had to keep pace. He increased the pace dramatically. Half of the platoon fell back, unable to maintain pace due to the added weight from the rucksacks.

Then we hit a huge hill that twisted and turned. He cranked it up even more. There were about ten of us left now. He maintained that pace, and it took everything I had to keep up with him. I was not going to let this man beat me even though he was in sneakers, shorts, and a T-shirt and I was in full gear with a huge pack on my back and carrying a weapon.

We got to the top of the hill and he sprinted down. He got a good twenty-yard lead on me, and I dug deep, put my head down, picked up my knees, and cranked it. I closed his lead to five yards. Once we hit flat ground, he maintained an insane pace and I was dying. I had snot exploding out of my nose and I was sucking wind, but I refused to quit. He maintained that pace for eight minutes, and I could start to hear him strain. It motivated the hell out of me, and I turned my brain off and kept up with him. We kept running for another five minutes side by side. He was breathing heavily. I just had to find a way to outlast him.

Luckily, I didn't have to. He pointed to a plateau and indicated that it was the finish. I took off in a dead sprint. He did too. We left the remaining two guys behind us. I beat him. I puked my guts out at the top and dropped to my knees. I puked again and used my rifle as a prop to get me back onto my feet. Despite the puke on my face and uniform, Drill Sergeant Valencia got an inch away from my face and screamed.

"*Where are your men?*"

I was fired on the spot.

Leadership

No one had ever beaten Drill Sergeant Valencia, and I should have felt absolutely incredible, but instead I was sick to my stomach. By putting myself above the platoon, I had failed miserably as their leader and deserved to be fired from my role as platoon leader.

I didn't do it on purpose, and I can't imagine a scenario in which I would ever knowingly put myself above those I lead. I take the job too seriously. When you're in charge, it's your job to put the needs of those you lead above your own. I had been doing it for years and had won dozens of leadership awards at the county, state, and national levels. I never assumed that I knew all there was to know about leadership. I was always hungry to listen and learn which is why I was effective and felt comfortable in a leadership position. I would never say that I was the best leader that I knew (far from it), but I was confident in my ability to help position those I lead so that they would succeed—so that *we* would succeed. I didn't have a perfect track record, but it was pretty damn good if we're being honest.

That race did a number on my confidence and on my ego. As it should have. I got suckered into disregarding the most fundamental leadership principle because I wanted to beat Drill Sergeant Valencia's ass. My drive to win was ironically what caused me to lose. It was a burning, acidic lesson in humility.

When we as men are in leadership positions, we must never allow the power, prestige, and opportunities for personal advancement to conflict with our duty to serve those we lead. That doesn't mean that we do not take advantage of the perks of leadership. If done **responsibly and ethically**, we should feel no shame or hesitation to leverage our responsibilities for personal growth, advancement, etc. But these things can never happen at the expense of those we lead. That is completely unacceptable.

I deserved to be fired on the spot. I had failed in my basic duty to secure the whereabouts of my men at all times. It is akin to just running away and leaving them behind. The fact that Drill Sergeant Valencia baited me meant nothing. I tripped on temptation. It was my fault. I couldn't blame him. I knew better.

I carry that lesson with me every day and try to keep my responsibilities at the forefront of my mind instead of my desires. Should you assume a leadership position, I strongly recommend that you do the same. Execute your duties to the best of your ability. As your ability to execute your duties improves, you'll be amazed at how personal advancement seems to happen organically. You'll most likely receive greater roles and responsibilities, which also carry greater privilege. Momentum builds. This all rests on a thorough understanding of what you are called to do while in a leadership position, which is to **serve others**. Only with this understanding in place can you fully commit to do your duty to the best of your ability.

Imagine what the world would become if all our leaders honored this basic principle: **duty before desire.**

Someone Is Always Watching

The drill sergeants are clever in how they punish other guys for your mistakes. They'll drop the whole platoon to the dirt and sweat them out while they make you stand still and watch. They single you out for negative behavior and punish the guys around you. So, when Drill Sergeant Valenta would constantly remind us that "someone is always watching," most guys took it as a warning. It took me a while, but I eventually realized that it held another meaning.

At some point during training, I was asked to coach the entire platoon on how to shoot. Then, shortly after, other drill sergeants from other platoons asked me to work with their soldiers as well. They asked me to do the same thing with basic breathing tips so that guys could complete the bare minimum two-mile run test time requirements. I had no idea why this was happening, but then I realized that Drill Sergeant Valenta had seen me coaching up guys. The "someone is always watching" also meant that the drill sergeants were actively looking for soldiers who were trying to do the right thing because of the inherent value in doing the right thing. I got *caught*. Ironically, I was given rank, more responsibility, and higher value privileges as a result.

It stuck with me forever and is something that we, as men, must always carry with us. In some form or another, someone is watching us. If you know that and interpret it only as a hypervigilant eye looking to catch wrongdoing, you'll do just enough to not get in trouble. If you interpret it as an opportunity for growth, you'll go above and beyond what is expected of you because you trust that eventually you will get noticed for doing something well. It positions your efforts differently. **One approach is punitive, the other is opportunistic.**

I've incorporated this idea into my mentoring style with great success. As men, if we look to acknowledge the good in each other, we will eventually bring out the best in each other as well.

Someone is always watching.

"You Are Going to Struggle"

2012

I eventually did regain leadership of the platoon and was chosen to be the guidon bearer during our graduation ceremony. That meant I held our company flag and stood next to our captain in front of brigade leadership and anyone else who came to watch graduation. All other soldiers and drill sergeants stood behind us. Drill Sergeant Valenta won Drill Sergeant of the Cycle, and I was a co-winner for Soldier of the Cycle and sole winner for guidon bearer. Holding the flag and being chosen to represent our company at graduation was a tremendous honor.

My folks and sister came to graduation. Despite our broken family, everyone was sober, respectful, and patriotic, even if only for the moment.

Before I was given permission to leave the base, I sprinted back into our barracks to find Drill Sergeant Valenta. I wanted to thank him. I broke the rules and knocked on the door by myself. No one else was around. He ordered me in. I asked him for permission to speak freely and he granted it. I thanked him. Afterward, he had something to say to me.

"DAGS, sit down."

I was in shock. He had never called me by any name whatsoever, and to hear him call me by my nickname was surprising. I sat down and listened to him. He told me that he recognized my dad from the crowd despite having never met him or seen a picture. He said we looked alike. He asked me questions about my family and my upbringing. I answered all his questions succinctly and honestly.

He took a deep breath, rubbed his hands on his face, and broke his drill sergeant bearing. He looked me right in the eyes and spoke to me like a human being.

"DAGS, listen to me. You are going to struggle. I'm sorry."

Basic training had gone beautifully. I was the platoon leader, co-winner of Soldier of the Cycle, guidon bearer, and rated in the top 1 percent of entry-level soldiers. I was off to a great start, and I loved being a soldier.

It then knocked me for a loop to hear Drill Sergeant Valenta tell me I was going to struggle at Officer Candidate School (OCS) where soldiers trained to become commissioned officers. He explained to me that my only shot to thrive in the Army was either in Special Forces or Military Intelligence. He said the way I mentally approached missions and tasks, although effective, would not align to the way OCS or the Army did things. He also told me it was not a good time to be at OCS, which echoed what every other military advisor had told me as well.

The reason was that we were downsizing from two wars overseas, and officers are expensive. The Army was trying to get rid of financial weight, and rules were changing rapidly. By the time I got to OCS, the rule was if you got injured, you would be discharged. This discharge didn't apply to just OCS, but from the Army entirely. Get hurt and you're out for good.

Unfortunately, I got injured at OCS. Drill Sergeant Valenta's prophecy then became a reality. I struggled. The two things that I had been warned not to do by all my military advisors ended up being the two things that happened—I got *injured* and entered *Army bureaucracy*.

Anyone who has served knows that despite how positive and life-changing the Army can be, Army bureaucracy is not where you want to be. It is the Wild West. Anything can happen.

During any other time, my injury would have been treated and fixed, and I would have then gone through OCS. But in that political climate, they medically discharged me. I had done everything I could to escape my family situation and pursue a better life. I had prepared my body to deal with the rigor of training. I had mentally prepared myself to deal with toxic leadership if I came across it. I loved being a soldier, serving our country and being part of something bigger than me. I always knew I was going to serve, and I had bet my entire future on it. But I was discharged in less than six months.

I lost it all. I was gutted—completely and utterly devastated. The shame was overwhelming.

I returned home, and the following year was the darkest of my life. It marked the culmination of a decade of personal failures, and a re-immersion into an abusive home. I was incapable of processing anything. The fallout from the loss of the flag on my arm was severe. I had loved the Army. It gave me more than I could have ever dreamed of—identity, camaraderie, pride, and purpose.

I was barely in my body and carried nothing but pain in my heart. I was not permitted to work through it because the toxicity at home was too intense. The situation had intensified and escalated to the point that I was in real danger most nights. The shame was equally dangerous. I'm not sure which was worse.

I was not a student, an athlete, a son, or a soldier. Without the flag on my arm, I thought that I wasn't a man. I didn't know who I was or what I was supposed to be. I had no identity.

I was aimless.

Redefining Masculinity and Embracing the Journey

It was the discharge that took me to rock bottom. Every single belief system that I carried was challenged and, in many cases, discarded. I stopped taking care of myself. I stopped training hard. I started drinking in excess—again. I jumped right back to my old ways with women and was immediately reminded of its perils with yet another terrible experience. Out of desperation, I dove deeper into my faith and started reading my notes and texts more fervently. Sadly, I wasn't getting much out of them. I had too much pain in my head and couldn't focus. To make spiritual matters worse, my mother found my journals and wrote monstrous things all over them.

The entire experience was invasive, and not a single part of my life felt safe or good.

My sense of self was gone. I had no guiding principles to follow. None of my decisions were aligned to my identity because I no longer knew who I was. The aimlessness was dangerous. Without a true north, I lost my way and fell into depression, much deeper and darker than the depression I had experienced years earlier. It was terrifying.

As personal as ten years of consecutive failures with women, family, military service, autonomy, finances, health, etc. was for me, many men go through something similar in their own way. The failure to meet toxic male standards leaves one feeling shamed. Even when men meet masculine standards, they are then taught to be even more of a *man*. The effort it takes to be a "man" does not provide a meaningful return, and because the socially accepted traits of masculinity are so destructive, many are ashamed to express their masculinity in any way whatsoever.

However, we cannot remove the male identity entirely simply because of the rotten traits within it. I understand that many mistakes have been made, so many have gotten hurt, and people are saying screw it. After so much failure and loss, that's what I did. The result was catastrophic. Without an identity, men are aimless. Aimlessness is a huge problem, and its negative effects bleed into all components of the male experience, especially mentally.

I believe wholeheartedly that the majority of the mental health crisis in men is primarily created by a baseless devotion to toxic interpretations of masculinity, and society's attempts to "cleanse" masculinity altogether. **It leaves a lasting impression on men that they either aren't man enough, or they aren't a man at all.** Neither sentiment is effective, and both leave men broken.

I've been on both sides of that coin and understand why some may want a male identity and some don't. You'll find no judgment from me if someone feels either way. But my hope is that we can all collectively and consciously choose to educate and support people by showing the value in creating a constructive male identity— one that builds men up and brings beauty into their lives and into the lives of others.

Being a man must lead to a state of being that is desirable and beneficial to everyone. The pursuit of a constructive male identity needs to lead to opportunities which can help men craft a beautiful life. They need to be consistently successful within those opportunities as well. We cannot continue to engage in ineffective, misguiding behaviors nor can we abandon the pursuit of manhood altogether by a metaphorical neutering. We must do something different, something better.

Instead of removing the male identity or forcing a toxic interpretation, we can instead embrace the journey to masculinity and allow it to be individualized and unique to the person.

Each path to becoming a man is different. But like all journeys, there is failure, uncertainty, and moments of weakness. Those are predictable adversities anytime we challenge ourselves, but they are far more likely to happen when uncovering our identities as individual men. It is not a path meant to be walked alone. Men need direction and safe environments to talk about the things they experience without fear of being judged, being labeled a pussy, or having masculinity physically beaten into them. This is where having a guide, a *mentor*, can make all the difference.

As fate would have it, I was about to meet a man whose mentorship would change the course of my life forever.

Charity

2013

It was summer of 2013, and over the course of an eight-year skid, I had failed in every professional pursuit, lost many relationships, been medically discharged from the Army, and battled domestic abuse, and my family deteriorated to the point that police and the courts had to get involved. I was dead broke, struggling with alcohol abuse, and suffering from severe panic disorder, PTSD, and depression. I was desperate for a break in a storm that seemed to never end. My life outlook was bleak.

Luckily, Mr. and Mrs. C took me into their home while I looked for a job. Despite being down and out and knowing full damn well that I needed to accept their kindness, my ego still punished me. My whole life I had believed that a man must always be self-sufficient, never showing weakness or accepting assistance from others. Every night I slept on the floor in the room they provided me. I didn't feel I deserved a bed and was nauseous with self-disgust. Despite those feelings, I continued to accept their generosity. The reality was that I had no other options.

For months, I had no luck getting interviews despite applying to dozens of companies. Few people were successful getting hired during that time. I had to hustle and do whatever I could to earn money. Landscaping and personal training were my primary revenue sources, but they were inconsistent and low paying. It was another blow to my ego to be an Ivy League graduate who served in the Army yet still be unable to land a job. I couldn't pay my bills. I was living on someone else's charity. I felt ashamed to no longer be in uniform. Drill Sergeant Valenta's prophecy came true—I was struggling.

I just finished working on someone's yard when I saw that my dad had left me a voicemail. He said that a man by the name of Gene Miller was interested in talking to me. Gene was a former Top Gun pilot and Naval Academy graduate. "Gene is a *good man*," he said. The title of "good man" was not something that my dad assigned regularly. When I called my dad back, he told me that Gene was expecting me in Clay Hamlin's office (a very good friend of my father and another *good man*) that same afternoon. I balked at that initially because I was sweaty and dirty, which I felt would make a terrible first impression.

"Don't worry about it. Gene is coming from the tennis court. He just wants to talk to you."

I drove over to Clay's office despite having never met Gene or done anything like this before. I couldn't make sense of how this was going to work out. How was I supposed to know who he was? I didn't have his personal contact information and had no idea what he looked like. What were we going to talk about? Why did he want to talk to me at all? It was a bizarre situation but oddly comical. I had nothing better to do, so I went in blind.

Shortly after entering Clay's office, his administrator led me to a cubicle in the back. I waited for a minute or two and then Gene walked in. He didn't walk like anyone else that I had ever seen—it was more like a march combined with a careless, happy-go-lucky stroll. He was roughly six feet tall, clean cut, and visibly fit in his tennis clothes. Gene had great energy and looked like he belonged on stage.

"JohnnyD! I played golf with your father last week. We talked and I told him I had to meet you."

Gene was genuine and disarming. My worry over a poor first impression quickly subsided. We chatted about sports, UPENN, and coaching amongst other things. I was shocked that I had never met him prior to this meeting because apparently we swam in the same waters. I also liked him right way. There was nothing not to like. He was respectful and insightful and created a safe space to talk about topics that I wouldn't discuss with anyone else, especially those that were military-related.

I was a medical drop from the Army, which carries enough dishonor in and of itself. To make matters worse, my discharge was training-related. It wasn't even from combat. In my mind, that made my discharge shameful and completely unrelatable to those who have never served. Luckily, he understood and even detailed his frustrations with military structures and protocols, which mirrored my own. I hadn't talked to anyone in depth about my discharge experience up until that point. He had an outstanding military record yet understood my situation perfectly. Even if only for a moment, it felt like I could drop the shame I carried.

"You reek of character," he said.

I burst out laughing. Gene had a great sense of humor and an ability to deliver a joke at the perfect time. He cleverly acknowledged the fact that I smelled awful and also that I tried to do the right thing during my military discharge process.

While laughing, I quietly said, "Thank you, Gene. Means a lot."

"Listen Johnny, we don't currently have any positions open: full-time, part-time, or intern. But I want you to come work for me on our CITRS initiative. I can't pay you, but I think it would be good for you."

CITRS was an acronym for Character-Integrity-Trust-Relationships-Success. The company mantra was, *"If you have character and integrity, people will trust you. And if people trust you, you will have great relationships in your life. And relationships are the foundation for success in everything that you do."* It made perfect sense to me. Gene went on to describe the company mission and vision and how we would be focusing on scaling character education to grades K–12. I was deeply interested, but I knew that there was no way I could take an unofficial position. I needed money urgently. Working for beans wasn't going to cut it.

"Take some time to think it over, and we'll talk in a week or so."

Despite my intense interest, my answer could only be no. I couldn't take a job for no pay. It was as simple as that. I did as many calculations as I could to try and persuade myself to work for Gene, but all number crunching pointed to an impossibility.

On the morning of the day I was scheduled to call Gene, I got two unexpected emails. Both emails offered me full-time, low-paying jobs with potential paths toward lucrative pay built into the offers at two different reputable companies. Now I had options. It made the decision a no-brainer. I received two fantastic opportunities, but a lump still formed in my throat. I still had to tell Gene.

I called and after I told him about the job offers, Gene offered me sincere and genuine congratulations. He was truly excited for me and told me that I'd be great in either role. He asked me which one I was leaning toward, and

I told him. He believed it was the right decision and assured me that there were no hard feelings. All he asked was that we keep in touch.

Gene didn't know that I was in a dark place and that his kindness was overwhelming. I took a deep breath and could not believe that I was about to say no to this man, but there was nothing else I could say. I had made all the calculations and looked at it from every angle. I just needed to steel myself, say no thank you, and hang up.

Instead, I said, "Gene, I want to come work for you."

Building Legacies of Charity in the Workplace

I found out later that I wasn't the first young man that Gene took under his wing. He had been mentoring soldiers at the United States Naval Academy for decades, and sometimes he helped young men who had lost their way. Not only was it clear that I was aimless, it was also obvious from a distance that I wasn't "right." I had weird energy to me, an unkept appearance, and at times a sour attitude. Gene was compassionate and saw through all of that. He gave me a chance to prove that I was serious about working, and I was a "yes sir, no sir" type worker for *him*. Although I had to eat my pride to accept his kindness, I still felt I owed him something for seeing through my storm and holding me accountable to a better way of life. I did whatever he told me to the best of my ability.

Weeks later, CITRS opened a part-time intern position and offered me $12 an hour. I accepted the offer immediately.

I hope that businesses (more specifically the people within them) will make an active effort to extend work opportunities to young men regardless of what they look like, where they come from, or their status in life. The willingness to work and learn comes in all shapes and sizes, and businesses can promote young men in ways they can't imagine.

I would ask businesses to also consider the impact they can make on the lives of young men by extending opportunity to places off the beaten path. There is something to be said for pursuing candidates with prestigious colleges and work histories on their resume. There is certainly value there. But I can confidently say from my own time spent mentoring young men with rough personal histories, there is nothing quite like a young man who is hungry to work and improve himself. These young men will run a mile over broken glass to honor opportunities given to them. Not only that, but they'll pass the kindness and compassion they received on to others out of a sense of gratitude.

If businesses are willing to look at their purpose a little differently, it will become obvious that they can do more than drive the financial bottom line. They can also generate personal growth and legacies of compassion by extending opportunity to young men who need a chance.

For some men, pride can lead them to think that they *should* be granted chances just because they are a man. For other men, pride prevents them from accepting charity from others. Lastly, and perhaps most egregious, pride can make some men hoard their blessings. However, *gratitude* can push those deformed beliefs out of the masculine identity.

Gratitude is one of the most powerful virtues that a man can have. It allows us to acknowledge the things we have that some don't, feel thankful for them, and willingly extend charity toward others who are less fortunate.

My dad stuck his neck out for me, Mr. and Mrs. C gave me a roof over my head, and Gene offered me a learning curve. Not everyone has those privileges. I was aware of it, and no matter how much my ego tried to shame me at night, my sense of gratitude for their kindness overpowered all the self-hatred I carried. I had a man to call "Dad," a safe place to live, and a meager paycheck. Altogether, it was **a chance to better myself.** Masculine pride be damned, I intended to make the most of that opportunity and pass their charity to others I met along the way.

Used Paper and Broom Closets

The internship at CITRS started out with basic "lay of the land" responsibilities—file this here, learn that there, get to know this person there, etc. From the get-go, it was obvious that I was going to be at the bottom of the hierarchy, which didn't bother me at all. The team was made up of aces, and I was excited to have an opportunity to learn from them.

First there was Gene, the president and cofounder of CITRS. He was a United States Naval Academy graduate and ethics professor, tennis player and coach, Top Gun pilot, war veteran, and volunteer mentor. He was, as my dad put it, a *good man.*

Clay was the CEO and cofounder of CITRS, a UPENN graduate and tennis player, navy veteran, businessman, and philanthropist. Clay partnered with Gene to cofound CITRS as a way to give back. He was easygoing, generous, and a bottomless pit of knowledge.

Jeanne was the VP of CITRS. She was a tennis player and strengths development coach, was a positive psychologist, and spent her free time mentoring young women playing racquet sports at Ivy League schools. Jeanne had the most calm and safe energy about her. Her extensive professional experience working with people from all backgrounds gave her unique perspective.

Brendan was VP of client relations, did curriculum, and had a host of other responsibilities. He had worked as an educator for over twenty years with leadership experience in many different academic environments. Brendan lent immediate credibility to CITRS from an educator perspective. Although Gene was in charge of my development, Brendan was my direct report. We clicked right away. He was a blast to work with and taught me about curriculum design, lesson structure, and youth education practices.

Then there was me, the runt of the litter in my ways—an intern, UPENN grad, two-sport Division I athlete and semipro baseball player with brief military service. On paper, there wasn't much I could contribute to CITRS other than my work ethic and roughly ten years (at the time) of experience working with youth as a camp counselor/director and sports coach. As early as sixteen, I found that I had a passion to work with kids, and CITRS aligned to those values.

Gene leveraged that passion and taught me about character education and performance protocols. He would deliberately overload me with work to see how I would react, and then coach me afterward. It was like drinking through a firehose and I loved it. Within three months, he taught me to work at such a speed that I became everyone's "shift" man. Essentially, whatever grunt work they all had was funneled to me, and I'd process it and return it back to them. By doing that, it allowed me to learn more about their responsibilities and expertise, and it positioned them to focus their efforts on more high-value targets. We made a great team.

With the busywork jobs out of the way, I had earned trust and was given bigger responsibilities that initially required more tutelage. Gene and Brendan taught me about lesson planning and creation, and they gave me a crack at writing three lessons based off the key takeaways that they provided from the CITRS curriculum designed by Gene. It was a new skill, so it took me a while. But they turned out okay.

There were close to one hundred lessons remaining that needed to be written, designed, and completed with media sources, quotes, and additional materials. It was a massive undertaking.

It was the tail end of spring, and Gene, as he loved to do, challenged me.

"JohnnyD, you have until the end of the fall to write the remaining lessons. I bet you can't do it."

That gave me just under six months to do a year's worth of work. Using prioritization and process (performance principles that Gene taught me), I finished them in under three months.

Brendan was wide-eyed and Gene couldn't stop laughing when I told them I was done. It had earned me a spot on the trip up to New York City to present to a potential partner.

CITRS specialized in curriculum design, training the trainer, and consulting. We would partner with organizations, the vast majority of which were schools and non-profits. This particular trip was to present our curriculum and program to a massive non-profit called New York Junior Tennis and Learning (NYJTL), which was amongst the largest non-profits in the city.

With no warning whatsoever, fifteen minutes before we were to present to over fifty NYJTL mid-level leaders and top-level executives, Gene pulled me aside.

"JohnnyD, I'd like you to present the bulk of the curriculum design and lesson structure and take the group through two lessons yourself. That shouldn't be a problem for you, correct?"

My jaw was on the floor. I was completely unprepared and thought I was going to be a silent observer for this trip. Now I was tasked with representing CITRS in front of people I had never met, and Clay was watching!

I basically blacked out in the hallway and hyper-focused myself on our materials and agenda for the day. Surprisingly, my presentation went well enough that Clay and Gene agreed to bring me on as full-time employee. In under twelve months, I went from intern to Associate Editor and from there was promoted to Assistant VP of Product Development.

Despite the promotions, my financial troubles were very real. I was in the hole for tens of thousands of dollars and unable to get financial assistance. I had no idea that the money I had given to my mother to pay off my student loans was used to fund addictions. The string of missed payments obliterated my credit score to the point that I couldn't get a $50 line of credit. The damage was severe. I was financially immobilized. I read many books and scoured the internet to learn as much as I could about personal finance.

Luckily, CITRS was sandwiched between Clay's corporate real estate business and investment firm. I sat next to the office accountant, Hugh, who handled numbers for the multi-operational office. Hugh freely shared some basics about budgeting that were essential to complement my personal finance self-education.

With my new financial knowledge, I calculated that I would have to live on a $7 a day budget for a minimum of two years if I wanted to have any credit and get out of the hole. It was incredibly challenging, demoralizing, and difficult to explain to anyone without going into detail about my family situation, which I wasn't willing to do. Despite working four jobs—CITRS, bartending, bouncing, and personal training—I still missed out on many important events with dear friends, like weddings and bachelor parties, because I couldn't afford it. I felt like a terrible friend.

Yet because of the nature of the work at CITRS, I never regretted it. We had landed partnerships in Buffalo, Philadelphia, Baltimore, and New York City. I was meeting tons of really interesting people and entering dozens of businesses and schools, and the curriculum that I wrote was being scaled to thousands of kids, most of whom I was able to meet in person. It was an amazing experience.

Brendan insisted that CITRS have a "presence and a pulse" with all partners, especially schools and community centers. So, he and I would visit each location ourselves. We spent countless hours on the road together and looked forward to these trips with great excitement. We had become great friends and didn't mind the travel.

Because CITRS partnered with organizations that covered the entire socioeconomic spectrum, we got the chance to work with everything from incredibly wealthy prep schools to poor community centers. Each client was different, but the routine remained the same. Brendan and I would drive there, meet the leader(s) of the location, be given a tour, present a lesson to the kids, and chat with the employees or volunteers of the location depending on the nature of the site.

While the wealthy largely focused on competing for spots at top-level universities, the underprivileged had more immediate concerns—like where they could get their next meal or sleep safely that night. This was reflected in our debriefings with the leaders of each location. The leaders at wealthy locations cited things like graduation rates and percentages of students attending top ranked universities. The leaders in poorer locations told us about how many of their kids were below the poverty line and subject to gang violence. We got tours of magnificent facilities with the wealthy, and we were coached about where to park, where not to drive, and how to get to the highway before sundown by those working in underprivileged areas.

I remember going to a wealthy site and waiting for the Wi-Fi password before continuing the presentation in a multimillion-dollar facility and in that same month, giving a presentation to poor students **on used paper in a broom closet.** I'd return to my apartment after visiting underprivileged areas like that and just sit and stare at the wall in darkness. I couldn't believe that there were these microclimates in otherwise iconic American cities where neighborhoods are so poor and gang violence so high that community representatives would feel a sense of responsibility to ensure that Brendan and I could enter and exit safely while still taking care of the kids in their programs.

Those microclimates were rough. Often these neighborhoods had deteriorated to the point that windows were broken, steps were crumbling, potholes were everywhere, and businesses were boarded up. Gas station clerks always sat behind bulletproof glass. The areas were desolate and dangerous, especially after sundown when the gangs would come out. But the community centers were safe. They were often set up in buildings that had been repurposed to become mini schools for summer programming for the kids. Although driving in and out could be a little gnarly, being in the community centers themselves was truly a gift.

As a former teacher, Brendan would always remind me to look at the walls when inside a site. More specifically, he'd ask me to soak in the artwork and take particular notice of whether or not students respected each other's creative expressions. Meaning, look to see if the artwork was untouched and celebrated or covered in graffiti and torn down.

Amazingly, the art was always untouched. Not only that, but it was also absolutely beautiful! Their talent was extraordinary and their self-expression unmatched. Although the facilities in wealthy neighborhoods were awe-inspiring, I fell in love working with the underprivileged. They showed remarkable resilience, creativity, and camaraderie. They also made no effort to put up a front. They were honest and expected me to be honest as well. That was the only expectation really—honesty. Kids are kids. They demanded authenticity and would tune out even the most buttoned-up presentation if they sniffed an inkling of artificiality or salesmanship. By being vulnerable and real, we could connect.

When Brendan and I would finish our presentation, Brendan would go with the community leaders and volunteers to have teacher-talk, leaving me with the kids. I'd ask them if they had any questions, and this is when I knew I was in for it. Before each presentation, Brendan would introduce me and tell the kids that I served in the Army, was an athlete, etc. Based on this information, the questions that followed after the other adults left were absurd. They wanted to test me to see how I would handle myself, especially the teenagers. They'd often take their demands of honesty a bit too far, and I couldn't help but play along. It always shocked them with how I answered.

"You a virgin?"

"Italian. Thank you for asking."

"You ever killed somebody?"

"Not today."

I usually could get a chuckle out of them and put them at ease. Then it would be my turn to ask questions, and having been in this position many times before, I had questions holstered and at the ready. I would usually start with something easy like who is your favorite musician, what is your favorite movie, etc. Then I'd work them toward questions that were more substantive.

"Who do you want to be?"

I was always interested in their responses because more often than not, they'd respond with a title or profession. They would rarely, if ever, describe human traits like kind, hardworking, or inventive. This allowed me to take full advantage of the moment and reframe their responses.

"Let's try this: what personality traits do you think you need in order to become what you want to become?"

This question helped them highlight the behaviors they felt would be necessary, and to ideally use those behaviors on a daily basis to align their growth to their future goals. The discussions that followed these types of questions were nothing short of brilliant, and I could often see their eyes opening right in front of me.

This day, Brendan and the community volunteer came back into the room and told the kids it was time to take a break and play outside. Unprompted, most if not all the kids said, "Thank you, Mr. John," as they walked out the door and asked me if I would come play outside with them. I took offers like this as a tremendous compliment and joined them, no matter the weather. With summer visits in New York City, the heat could be no joke. I'd ride home with Brendan covered in sweat.

In this instance, I remained in the classroom to organize our materials and put the space back in order before I joined them outside. I pushed in the chairs, cleaned the floor, and shaped it up in any way that I could. The chairs and desks made familiar sounds on linoleum floors, and I looked over the desks for graffiti and carvings. I wanted to know what these kids looked at and what they touched when they were in here. There wasn't anything too bad besides the occasional cuss word carved into a desk or two.

When I turned around, I saw a kid standing not too far away from me. I recognized him and remembered that he was pretty timid during our lesson and discussion. While everyone else was firing questions at me, he was quiet, slouched in his chair. But I could tell that he was paying attention. He never took his eyes off me. Even with his hood up, I knew that he had listened.

I said, "Ehi! Did you forget something?" but he didn't reply.

I waited a moment and then tried again, "You good?"

He just stood there. I was familiar with this. He wanted to talk but didn't have the confidence. I needed to make him feel comfortable, so I pulled out two chairs and faced them toward each other at a glancing angle. I sat in a chair to remove any possibility of my height intimidating him. I motioned him to the other chair, but he didn't move. I tried prompting him again.

"What's on your mind?"

He walked to the side of the seat but didn't sit down. He looked old for someone so young. I saw small dark circles on each of his eyelids. I didn't think much of it because these kids often drew on themselves with markers to mimic tattoos. He got closer and held his fist out in front of me. I could see more circles on his hand and neck, but they weren't from a Sharpie. I knew what they were, and it took my breath away.

He was covered in burn marks. Someone had branded him with cigarettes, even his face. My eyes welled up.

Still holding his fist out, he said, "I'll pray for you."

Tears poured down my face. "I'll pray for you too."

We fist bumped and he walked outside. I remained seated and cried.

Pity, Sympathy, and Empathy

I informed the site community leaders of what I saw, and they were well aware of the young boy's situation and were on top of it. It put me at ease, but when I got home that night I couldn't sleep. I just cried. I could not get the kid's face out of my head. At that point in my career working with underprivileged youth, I had never seen such obvious signs of child abuse. It was overwhelming.

When I first started working in underprivileged areas and saw the conditions the people live in and the sacrifices they have to make on a daily basis, my beliefs changed. Initially I felt pity, especially for the kids. However, the more that I got to know and work with them, pity became accompanied by *admiration*. Although their trials and tribulations are plentiful, I learned to not allow the injustices they've experienced and the pain they carry to dissuade me from calling on their potential. **Pity does not promote growth.**

I accepted that truth and chose to instead focus my emotional energies **by acknowledging and calling upon these young men's talents and positive behaviors.** Through this approach, I was able to hold them to their potential as I would for any other young man without presenting myself as ignorant or insensitive to the realities of their daily lives.

All children require emotional support, but there is a glaring disparity of resources and opportunities for children in underprivileged areas versus children in wealthy areas. Wealthy areas have well-established tracks that catapult kids to other places, but it's a different ball game altogether in underprivileged areas that require young people to make their *own* tracks with far less support—if any. The correlation between "work ethic" and "success" then becomes relative when considering the range of resources and adversities that youth have and face. I focused on helping youth self-actualize on their own terms. I encouraged them to listen to their inner voices and cultivate their strengths despite what the world told them about themselves.

The freedom to be themselves allowed us to connect, and the truth became self-evident—**these young men are truly brilliant.** Their creativity, kindness, resourcefulness, and problem-solving abilities are limitless. The *school of hard knocks* forced them to develop skills that kids in resource-rich areas do not have and that they could never develop otherwise. When education is paired with emotional support, young men in rough areas can learn to position their hard-earned skills to their benefit—"benefit" being relative to their individual identity and reality.

As men, we can allow the emotions we feel to stir up the compassion necessary to promote altruistic action. In doing so, we can call upon the best in each other.

As a young person, I had difficulty managing myself in everyday life because of the invisible scars I carried. I couldn't escape them, and no one could see them but me. I learned early on that describing my experiences to someone didn't translate to their understanding or empathy. Trying to be vulnerable and expressing myself always got me hurt and forced me to learn how to hide my pain. Yet this humble kid had burning cigarettes put out on him for everyone to see. There was no hiding. He was forced to show his scars. And yet he was the one who reached out to me and told me that I would be in *his* thoughts and prayers. I had never seen strength like that before.

There are countless others who know pain, and yet very few of them make the conscious decision to bring light into the world like that young man did. His strength of spirit has stayed with me all these years later. It is moments like those that have led me to dedicate myself to mentoring young men. Background, neighborhood, and social status don't deter me. I don't care for any political terms or ideologies that people use to separate young men from one another. **We don't need more separation.**

As men, we must honor each other's identity and individuality, but assumptions we make about those who are different than us actively prevent interpersonal connection. If that kid and I blindly followed assumptions (as some do), it would have squelched empathy. He could have made common assumptions about me being white, and I could have made common assumptions about him being Black. But we didn't do that. We didn't hide behind terminology. Instead, we showed ourselves and we opened our hearts to each other. We connected because we extended each other empathy as fellow human beings.

Empathy is the most underutilized virtue amongst men, and without it, collective emotional intelligence (EQ) is severely limited. **Men practice sympathy but not empathy.** Sympathy is putting yourself in someone else's shoes and recognizing how *you* would feel in their circumstances. Sympathy validates *your* own attitudes and opinions, not theirs. It doesn't promote connection. It promotes the preservation of your *self*. **Empathy is putting yourself in someone else's shoes, recognizing how *they* feel, and making an effort when appropriate.** Empathy gives you an understanding of *someone else's* thoughts and emotions. Because of this, empathy promotes connection and can challenge your perspective. Sometimes it can shake up your own views and belief systems. Men too often run from this possibility because it's much easier to judge someone else and safeguard your *self* than to be accepting, vulnerable, and open-minded, which can threaten your belief systems and require an effort.

To boil it down: Sympathy can make you feel better about yourself. Empathy can make you uncomfortable with yourself. **Unless we are making a conscious effort to be empathic (and therefore uncomfortable), human nature will have us pursue the path of least resistance.** In this case, that would be sympathy, because it makes us feel comfortable and there isn't much effort required.

Empathy is what allows us to consider other people's reality, not just our own. It is important that men receive education about things like pity, sympathy, and empathy, because without that education, the urge to be "right" clouds our vision of other people's reality. But with that education, we can see their life's truths.

I made the conscious choice to challenge my perspectives and learn how to build up the virtue of empathy because Gene and Brendan would always encourage me to walk a mile in someone else's shoes. Our road trips to all those different sites allowed me to practice empathy with an incredible range of diversity. That practice is what allowed me to effectively **build relationships with those that were different than me.** I wouldn't have been able to do my job without being empathetic.

Without empathy, we can't connect. Without connection, there is no growth. If we men continue to be blindly loyal to our reality and unwilling to consider other people's reality, we will continue to judge and divide. **Empathy is how we can bridge gaps and unite.**

Beer Muscles

2013

By 1:00 a.m., shoes stick to the floor. College kids pour in through the door for the late-night drink special found upstairs in the night club. The girls are covered in makeup and showing as much skin as possible. The boys arrive in large numbers wearing too much cologne and chewing mint gum. Everyone scrambles to the bar for drinks.

I graduated college years ago and don't belong here anymore. And yet I am here. I bounced for the bar months earlier and remained friendly with the service staff who never charged me for draft beer. I like to drink alone in the corner far away from the hustle and close to the employee space so it looks like I'm still one of the team. They crank up the music, which makes the kids shout to each other. It was deafening and I found it soothing not to hear my own thoughts. I came here often. It helped me sleep.

The local college football team was there getting loaded. There were some big guys swelling up and making sure no one trespassed on their turf. I avoided these guys. I assumed they recognized me because I denied several of them for fake IDs. I also tossed a few out. These guys rarely made it out without some sort of incident or drama. They were more dramatic than the girls and made me think of a song lyric by Jay-Z. "You know the type: loud as a motorbike but wouldn't bust a grape in a fruit fight."

I could see one muscle head on the far side of the bar. He was dancing with some girls and looked like he was used to having all eyes on him. His voice was so loud and cut through the music and the crowd. He kept screaming, "*Are you not entertained?*" over and over. I could tell the night was going nowhere good with this asshole around and that I should go. I wanted to hit the pisser before I left and decided to use the downstairs restaurant bathroom. It took me a while to sift through the nightclub crowd, which was packed. Once I did, I got down the steps and through to the restaurant bathroom quickly.

When I came out, the muscle head had somehow moved his dance party downstairs into the restaurant presumably to get drinks with no lines. I could see him clearly now, and he was visibly intoxicated. He was also massive at six foot eight, weighing at least 285 pounds. He looked like he lived in the weight room. I was a six foot four, 220-pound stick of butter and out of shape. I could handle myself in a scrap but knew the best course of action was to avoid an altercation with this guy. As I was just about to walk around him, he stumbled and fell into me, slamming me against the wall. I didn't react and asked him if he was good. He responded by shoving me into the wall again and then getting up in my face. He reeked of cheap vodka and Red Bull. His eyes looked cartoon-like.

I put my hands up and told him I was heading out. After I turned and walked away, he gave me a cheap shot from behind which sent me stumbling into the high-top tables, which they stacked against the wall to make room for the crowd. It sent all the drinks to the ground. He spun me around and pushed me into more tables, and I heard the wooden table legs groan against the floor. More kids were coming into this bar for drinks, and I could hear them all making comments about what they were witnessing. It was becoming a scene. I spotted the door on the other side and just wanted to leave.

This guy's speech was slurred, and he was spitting on me as he talked. His hands were gripping my shirt while my hands were at my sides. He was escalating quickly, and the people around him knew it. They were grabbing him and telling him to let go. The girls were telling him to walk away, and his teammates were shouting, "Yo bro, be chill! Be chill!" repeatedly. I assumed their panic meant that they had seen him blow up before. Everyone around us was frozen and staring, waiting for someone to throw a punch.

I didn't say anything. I didn't change posture or energy. I went cold. Everyone was focused on him. No one knew that I had grabbed a bottle opener off the bar and had gripped the corkscrew between the fingers of my fist. I didn't hide it. I didn't have to. No one was looking at me. I just waited for him to do something stupid. I wanted him to hit me or push one of the girls, then I would punch the corkscrew into his throat and go to work on his eyes while he choked. I knew his eyes would bulge and then I could stab them with the corkscrew.

Still holding on to my shirt, he started jabbing my jaw with both of his fists. I had enough and waited for his elbows to spread apart enough for me to do what I needed to. I saw the opening, gripped the corkscrew, and was one breath away from maiming him for life, but then they pulled him off me.

I walked out.

I put the key into the lock of my apartment, opened and closed the door, and then sat down on the floor. My

90

dog Rocco slowly walked over, curled up, and fell asleep on my legs. I scratched his ears and neck and left my hand on his ribs. He would always take in a huge breath and then exhale slowly when we were reunited at the end of the day. I loved to hold on to his throat and feel him breathing under my hand with my other hand over his heartbeat. We did this every night.

I couldn't sleep, so I stared at the wall. I could still smell that guy's breath and see the heartbeat in his neck. Had I defended myself, I would have been arrested. I wasn't sure if I cared. Then I thought about my dad getting a call from the police. I could see his face dropping into his hands after the cops told him what I did. My eyes welled up.

I laid Rocco down gently, stood up, and poured all the alcohol in my apartment down the drain. I never went back to that bar again.

Self-Ownership and Violence

I reflected on that night for weeks. Looking at it through my dad's eyes offered a different perspective, which made me take what I thought was the right course of action: Get rid of the booze. Don't go back to that bar. But the more I thought about it, the more that I realized those were just the first steps. They were not enough. I kept asking myself why that guy would not leave me alone. I was drinking by myself. I didn't say a word to anyone. I didn't make eye contact. I literally went to the other side of the building on a different floor and magically he appeared outside of the bathroom and chose to start something with me. Why did I grab the corkscrew? Why was I willing to ruin my life just to turn some drunk guy's face to burger meat?

The evolution of thought was ongoing. At first, I was defensive. It was the drunk guy's fault. I was minding my own business. He was the aggressor. I had to grab the corkscrew because he was huge and I'd need it to defend myself. I kept telling myself these truths because I needed to relieve myself of any blame in the whole situation. Then I told myself that no one got hurt and it wasn't a big deal. I rationalized the whole thing. It was pretty easy.

This narrative went on for weeks, but there was this nagging feeling, like a stone in my shoe, that kept reminding me that I was missing the point. This wasn't an isolated incident. Trouble was following me in other areas of life as well. Booze and bars just seemed to increase my chances. So, I figured that there had to be something else that was manifesting these issues. I thought to myself, "Is it me?" After I asked myself that question, all other rationale was pushed out. It was obvious. It was me. I couldn't lie to myself anymore.

My life had fallen apart. I had to take complete ownership of myself and right the ship. The first thing to go was excessive alcohol consumption and hanging out in high-drama environments. Clearly, bad habits and bad crowds was a recipe for drama. The next action item was wrangling my ego. Because of all the adversity I had experienced and the self-destruction that I had inflicted upon myself, my ego was severely damaged. **In my attempt to build myself up during a time when I was continually being torn down, I unknowingly had promoted my ego and demoted my character.** Now my ego was loud and had too strong a voice. This hierarchy prevented me from learning from my mistakes and incentivized me to continue down the path I was on. A man's ego cannot be wrong.

I, like many young men, chose to disregard constructive behaviors because things weren't going my way. It seemed pointless to continue doing the *right* thing and made far more sense to do the right thing for *me*. Eventually, the picture came back into focus.

I saw how easy it was to be destructive and how little I received in return. When you're in crisis, it's hard to make a single good decision, let alone a string of good decisions over a long period of time. As it was for most of my transformational moments, the sense of pragmatism won the day. Listening to my ego and disregarding guiding life principles was keeping me down. I had to take the higher, more difficult road to build myself up if I wanted out.

To this day, I am so thankful for that night. It forced me to admit to myself that too much of my pain was self-inflicted. **I couldn't control all the things that happened to me, but I could control how I responded to them.** I could make conscious choices. My decisions needed to be better. I needed to prioritize my character above all else by focusing on building positive behaviors. I needed to pursue virtue again.

I could not allow my ego to be behind the wheel anymore. My ego made it seem like the world was conspiring against me, which is total garbage. No one is at the center of the universe. I realized that **only I was held accountable to my actions. I couldn't blame anyone else.** I had to take full ownership of myself.

By taking ownership of ourselves, i.e., our thoughts, feelings, and actions, we can not only make better decisions that build up our lives, but we can also play a vital role in preventing unnecessary violence that tears apart relationships, families, and communities.

Toxic masculinity exalts violence as the ultimate expression of masculinity and strength. It is remarkable how much of man's mental space is occupied with violent thoughts. It is so deeply engrained into toxic male culture that men account for the overwhelming majority of violent crimes. The statistics are staggering.

Crime	% Committed by Men
Homicide	93
Forcible Rape	99
Robbery	87
Aggravated Assault	77
Burglary	84
Arson	82
Violent Crime	80
Other Assaults	73

—*Federal Bureau of Investigation (FBI) Uniform Crime Reporting (UCR)*

Looking at these statistics, it's clear: Violence is not a people problem. It's a *male* problem. So many lives are negatively impacted by this one toxic male identity trait.

That's the tragedy of violence—it hurts everyone. Furthermore, it is most often senseless and avoidable. Ego may be fluffed through violence, but the sensation is fleeting and hollow. There is no real value. I could have torn that drunk guy apart, but all I would have gained is a jail cell, and I would have ruined my life in the process.

With that said, I fully understand men's primal inclination toward violence. I admit that it often feels natural. That's why things like sports and martial arts are so important. They teach men to channel their aggression constructively. However, not all men have access or interest in those channels and instead get swept up into the hype. Combine toxic masculinity's praise for violence with testosterone, emotional suppression, and social expectations, and it's no surprise that so many men are like powder kegs. Violence is disastrous for everybody. No one wins.

This is a crucial point where men can reframe their energies. Because violence is remarkably destructive, it does not serve a man to choose violence. It only detracts from life. There is no value in it. With this understanding firmly in place, men can redirect their energies toward self-construction and building up their surroundings—something that benefits everyone.

The Realities of Male Violence toward LGBTQ+

I was a bartender for years before I joined the Army. I worked at a country club, an upscale American restaurant, and a beat-up ol' Irish pub named Sligo. I worked Sundays at Sligo, and the morning brunches were always fast and the nights were super slow, so I loved when people would belly up to my bar and strike up a conversation at night. It made the shift go faster.

One night shift, a gay couple walked in, and I invited them to sit at the bar because I was the only service worker there. Their names were Ray and Eric, and we had a great time chatting and enjoying a lazy Sunday. After they were done, they paid their tab, left a solid tip, and thanked me for making them feel *safe.* "Safe" sounded odd so I asked them what they meant. They explained that they sometimes felt unsafe at bars and restaurants that were frequented predominantly by straight people. I thanked them for sharing that with me and we eventually became friends. But it always bothered me that even in today's day and age, they still felt the need to be hyper-vigilant at bars.

LGBTQ+ people have struggled to find safe spaces for decades. Years later, I learned about the 1969 Stonewall Riots that sparked the gay liberation movement. On June 28, the police raided the Stonewall Inn, a gay bar in New York City, one of many police raids against gay bars across the country. This time, the bar patrons fought back, inspiring protests across the country. It saddened me to think that after all the decades' worth of sacrifices activists and protestors made, Ray and Eric *still* could not take safe spaces for granted. The way that we enforce where and how someone can express their masculinity is restrictive, but safe spaces should be the rule, not the exception. **Every man has a right to be themselves**, and it is up to every man to protect that right.

Nearly fifty years after the Stonewall Riots, on June 12, 2016, a man shot and killed forty-nine people and wounded fifty-three more at a gay nightclub in Orlando, Florida. It is considered the deadliest incident in the history of violence against members of the LGBTQ+ community. This tragedy reinforces a sad reality.

Male violence is disproportionately inflicted upon members of the LGBTQ+ communities.

A report from the National Crime Victimization Survey 2017 (NCVS) states that members of the LGBTQ+ community are more than four times more likely to experience violent victimization in comparison to non-LGBTQ+ people. They are also six times more likely to experience violence from someone they know and two and a half times more likely to experience violence from a stranger. Making these statistics even more troubling is the fact that members of the LGBTQ+ community are *half* as likely to report the violence inflicted upon them when compared to non-LGBTQ+ people.

In some places (like bars), I have to keep my guard up to ensure I don't cross paths with men who feel they need to prove their manliness by fighting. Alcohol consumption can sometimes fire up that misguided predilection. I cannot stand it. It ruins any sense of enjoyment. However, I can drop it and just be myself in most places. That's a reality I get to enjoy. Ray and Eric's experiences and the statistics point to a different reality for members of LGBTQ+ communities and how they experience toxic masculinity.

The glorification of violence by those who follow toxic masculine ideologies essentially forces LGBTQ+ people to keep their guard up—*everywhere*. They have to be more leery of the people they know and the people they don't know than non-LGBTQ+ people. LGBTQ+ people also feel that they can't report the violence inflicted upon them for multiple reasons: they fear being judged or not believed by authorities, and they also can be reluctant to disclose their sexual orientation/identity to authorities because it may lead to future discrimination or denial of services.

The LGBTQ+ reality of constantly feeling unsafe is decidedly different than non-LGBTQ+ people's reality. Non-LGBTQ+ people (especially heterosexual men) must acknowledge the daily tragedy that toxic masculine beliefs have created for everyone, especially the unjust and unnecessary threat of violence toward LGBTQ+ people. Their reality is so different that in many cases they can't even get a drink at a bar.

Angels

2014

I put the phone to my ear and nervously listened to it ring. After a few seconds, I heard him pick up.

"JohnnyD!"

"Coach A! How's it going?"

Crack.

"Johnny, it is going great. How are you?"

Crack. Crack. Crack.

"I am great as well. I can hear the guys in the background. Fellas getting in some BP before you get going for the day?"

"You know it. All three cages are down. We have guys hitting in the cage, guys on the side of the cage working off the T, and guys getting some soft toss in."

Crack. Crack.

"Oh man, Coach, I miss that sound! I'd love to swing some lumber around just for fun."

"Come on in! The guys would love to meet you."

"That's why I'm calling, Coach. I have an idea for a training program that I want to run by you. It's a combo of sports training, military discipline principles, and leadership development. If you're interested, maybe the Angels can be the first guinea pigs."

"JohnnyD, say no more. We have a practice tomorrow morning at 7:00 a.m. I'll introduce you and then you can have them for one hour. We're about to get going here, so I'll see you tomorrow morning."

He hung up while I was mid-response. Con Aquilante, whom I always called *Coach A,* has taught character and life lessons to his private baseball teams for over twenty-five years. He is energy incarnate. His brain is a fountain that overflows with life wisdom and baseball instruction. Years earlier, he helped me with college recruiting and is arguably the best coach that I ever had. With Con, I couldn't do a "good job." *Good isn't good enough.* If you even said the words "good enough" or "mediocre" around him, he'd vomit in his mouth and correct you immediately. Con demanded excellence—not just in baseball, but in all aspects of life. That's what was required from his Angels, and every player was well aware that if you met those expectations, especially with things like effort, focus, and teamwork, then Con would bend over backward to help you out. Con's track record helping guys get into college, no matter their walk of life, was incredible. But he'd never stick his neck out for you if your character wasn't up to his standards. It didn't matter how good a baseball player you were. He made it crystal clear: character first.

Con made a huge impression on me when I played for him, and I wanted to make the most of the opportunity that he had just given me. I knew that I had to *wow* him. I couldn't just give the Angels a great workout. He had access to a million trainers. I knew that I couldn't just give them a talk. He had public speakers come in every year, and Con was an incredible public speaker himself. I knew that I had to be different while still providing something that exceeded his standards and aligned to his program's values.

Con is no bullshit, so I was not surprised when he cut

right to the chase and then hung up abruptly. I was flattered that he assumed that I was ready to start. Unfortunately, I wasn't.

I knew that my idea had potential. What I didn't know was what it would look like. I had never done it before. When I called him, I was hoping for a month to prepare. He gave me a couple hours. I spent the night visualizing how I wanted the next morning to go a thousand times over in my head. It was not a restful night's sleep, and I got out of bed at 3:30 a.m. I drove in the dark to the facility and made sure I was the first one in the parking lot. Their practice started at 7:00 a.m., which meant that most guys would get there at 6:30 a.m. and would be warming up on their own at 6:45 a.m. I was there at 5:45 a.m. That kind of thing meant the world to Con. He was a big believer in being the first to arrive and the last to leave if you were in a leadership role. I was offering the Angels a leadership program and needed to set the example from the start. Being the first to arrive was step one.

Despite my punctuality and a restless night spent in preparation, my nerves were out of control. I had never been nervous for any other performance in my life. I had played in tons of big games, always with a cool, calm, and collected mindset. No problem. I enjoyed that kind of pressure. It's why I played sports. Pursuing greatness with your teammates was exhilarating and exciting. This was different. I was by myself. I could not let this man down or tarnish the Angel's legacy. After my unexpected discharge from the Army, I desperately needed to find a light in my life. This was my chance.

That morning in the parking lot, my hands were shaking uncontrollably. I could not get my breathing under control. I was about to have a panic attack. I looked around and no one was there, so I let it happen. My chest tightened and my heart raced. I couldn't breathe. Tears poured down my face. Ten years earlier, I would have been in a true panic without any understanding of what was going on. By this point, I had a decade's worth of panic attacks and knew the drill. Despite their discomfort, I knew it would pass if I could breathe through it.

Luckily it passed, and I got my breathing under control. My hands stopped shaking. I dug deep into my focus practices and locked in. I was motionless, inhaling and exhaling slowly and visualizing everything from start to finish. I stayed that way until Con got there (I had even visualized his arrival). He parked next to the facility door and got out, so I did too.

"JohnnyD! Good morning! How are you, my friend?"

"Very excited. I appreciate you bringing me in."

"JohnnyD, I can't wait to see it. Are you ready? Do you need me to do anything?"

"Not a thing. Just put me in, Coach."

With that, he laughed his wonderful hearty laugh that had a tinge of Southern twang hidden amongst his Italian American background.

He opened the door and brought me in. He flicked on a few lights and they made loud clanging sounds roughly four stories above my head. They were the big-time lights needed to light an indoor soccer facility and would need time to warm up to full brightness. They were just a dull, pale orange for now. He had rented out the far end of the facility, which had enough space for a baseball infield. In Con's space, thick turf ran from wall to wall and it had those flecks of black tire rubber that jumped up when you hit the turf hard. Con had made the most of it. There were wires and clips everywhere. I could see multiple, huge batting cages folded against the wall on wire tracks at the far end. It was seriously impressive.

I said, "I can't wait to see the guys set this up, Coach. This is amazing."

"My son put up those wires. Aren't they something?"

"It's genius. The cages just slide in and out, yes?"

"Two minutes max."

"Incredible."

It felt good to be back in this kind of energy. The formula was simple. You came to Con to get better. Everyone worked. No one quit.

The players trickled in at first and then nearly all at once. They set their gear against the walls, and like Con said, the place was set up within minutes. He didn't instruct anyone to do anything. They just did it. Cages were out and everyone was jostling for reps before practice even started. It was a well-oiled machine.

I wasn't familiar with the space, so I walked around and assigned valuable details into my plans. The space itself was perfect for what I had in mind, and the miscellaneous equipment against the walls was easily usable. Whatever nerves I had were pushed out by intensity and laser-beam focus. Time slowed to a crawl.

I. Was. Ready. To. Go.

Con brought the guys together. They were standing close to us in a semicircle while he introduced me. Con gave them a brief overview of my sport, academic, and professional resume and shared a story about me when I was an Angel. In typical Con form, he told a helluva story and made me sound like I was a star. In other circumstances, I would have been complimented and possibly moved to tears. But in this moment, I was there on a mission. I didn't let any of it soak in. I maintained focus.

After he was done, he took a breath, smiled, and said, "JohnnyD, they're all yours."

I didn't say a word at first. Instead, I silently looked every one of them in the eye, moving from one player to another. Most glanced away. I took a step closer to the group. I was no more than a foot away from them, closer to them than they were to each other. Most of them were holding their breath. I extended my arm over and between their heads and pointed to their baseball bags against the wall in the far corner.

I whispered clearly and slowly, "All bags and equipment must be organized in a uniform manner. Wait for my command . . ."

I waited several seconds and then quietly said, "Move."

They started jogging to their bags with their backs to me. I took a big breath into my gut and barked, "*Move! Ten, nine, eight, seven, six, five, four, three, two, one, fail! Push-up position move!*"

Without hesitation, they all dropped into push-up position. It was too slow, so I ordered them back to their feet. Too slow again, back down to push-up position. I ordered them to their feet and back to me. This time they sprinted. Too slow. Push-up position move. On your feet. Too slow. Push-up position move. Ten seconds to organize your equipment in a uniform manner. Fail. Push-up position move. Push. Push. Push. Push. Push. Push. Push. Push. Push. Push. On your feet. Return to me. Too slow. Fail. Push-up position move. Push. Push. Push. Push. Push. Push. Push. Push. Push. Push. On your feet. Ten seconds to organize your equipment in a uniform manner. Fail. Push-up position move.

It was a breakneck pace which went on for fifteen minutes. Their equipment still had not been organized, and every one of them was sucking wind and bent over. I ordered them back to me.

"Men, that looked like a hot bag of trash. You will improve."

I took a deep breath and exhaled through my nose. I looked every one of them in the eye again. No one dared look away. The shock and awe had grabbed their full attention. The briefing began.

"My name is John D'Agostini. I am in charge of your training this morning. The rules are: You will give max effort and max focus at all times. You are held accountable to your actions or lack thereof. The sooner you realize that your decisions and indecisions affect others, the more effective a leader you could become. You will move with a purpose. No walking, unless otherwise instructed. You will support each other positively and build each other up. You will not say Can't, Won't, Quit, or Um or any derivative of Um. These are defeatist words and are not welcome in this program. Are there any questions?"

There were no questions.

"You have sixty seconds to hydrate in silence. Training is about to begin, men. Get your minds right. We have work to do."

For the next forty minutes, I drilled them nonstop. They had sweat dripping off the brims of their hats. Guys were dry heaving everywhere and a few were puking in the trash cans. I provided them with easy-to-complete missions if they could work as a functioning unit, but they were not on the same page. It was a shit show. Guys were running into each other, forgetting their own names, stuttering incorrect answers from layup questions. I had them crawling, turning, twisting, jumping, pressing, pulling, and doing every movement at my disposal within every inch of the space. They were sweating in areas of Con's space that they most likely never even knew existed. I forced them to take ownership of their space, and the cost was their blood, sweat, tears, and in some cases, vomit.

It frustrated them but I admired their competitive spirit. They never once quit or took their foot off the pedal. They heard "fail" a minimum of 250 times before we were done. I could tell that it pissed them off. In their eyes, the session was a catastrophic failure. For me, it could not have gone better. I was euphoric.

At the end of their training, I instructed them to drink water and then take a seat for our class session. At the beginning, I took off my watch and tossed it to one of the younger guys.

I said to him, "This presentation is sixteen minutes, and we will finish within thirty seconds. You are in charge of holding us accountable. Start the stopwatch."

I provided them with a lesson that I had been preparing for months, which discussed the enemies of a team—ignorance and apathy derived from selfishness—and how leaders can approach a process to eradicate those character traits from those they lead. They seemed engaged.

After I finished, I looked at the greenhorn young kid and said, "Stop the clock. What's our time?"

"15:50."

He returned the watch to me, and I asked them to stand up, thanked them for their time, and brought them in to break a huddle.

"*Get Some* on three. One, two, three . . ."

They shouted out in unison, "*Get Some!*"

Their battle cry echoed in the facility, and it gave me

goose bumps. I sent them to Con for the rest of their practice. They were wide-eyed and afraid to move.

Con got them going and pulled a handful of his older players over to speak with him privately on the side. I stood in the corner and drank from my water bottle. I had known Con long enough to expect that he would give me a post-performance assessment just like he used to when I played for him.

He came walking over to me like a coach walks to his pitcher from the dugout. His hair was silver and he was wearing his Angels gear. He put his hand on my shoulder and laughed quietly to himself.

"Johnny . . ."

He took a deep breath, got serious, and dropped his hand from my shoulder. He pointed his index finger and jabbed it into my heart in rhythm to the words he spoke.

"I have never seen anything like that in my life."

I nodded my head, unsure what to say. He spoke again. "No one can do what you do."

"I don't know about that, but thank you. I can get better."

"Johnny, I'm telling you. This is special. I want you here every weekend. I checked with the players. They agreed."

"Thank you, Coach. Yes sir. I'll be here."

Invictus was born.

To this day, what happened next never ceases to amaze me. I woke up at 3:30 a.m. for months to drive ninety minutes to work with the Angles first thing in the morning on weekends. Con paid me $15 per session, which was just enough to cover my gas and tolls, more than I could have asked for. Three of the Angels hired me to train them privately. They were my first three clients and years later would eventually get drafted by Major League

Baseball teams. While I was working with the Angels, parents outside of the organization had noticed that many of the boys I had been working with were starting to carry themselves differently. Their overall demeanor and maturity were appealing. Those parents then asked me to work with their sons. Within a few months, I was training players outside of the Angels organization in a physical training area that Con allowed me to utilize when his players were not in it. In exchange for using that space, I brought my weights and allowed the Angels to use it or even borrow it at their convenience. It was a character program. If I couldn't trust the Angels, I couldn't trust anyone. It was a great partnership.

A part-time weekend side hustle was born, and my clientele grew quickly to the point that I was heavily considering leaving my full-time job to take a crack at becoming a full-time entrepreneur instead. My girlfriend, who eventually became my wife, asked me to consider bringing my business idea to Minnesota, her home state. If not for the fact that I despised my full-time job, I would have rejected the idea. But by this point in my life, I had left CITRS, a high-impact mission, to pursue a more lucrative career. I found a job as an HR consultant and sales rep. It was purely profit-related. I did well, substantially increased my standing financially, and made wonderful relationships that last to this day. I can thank my boss and friend Rich Toland for my success there, but I knew that I didn't belong. It was spiritless work.

I agreed to visit Minnesota and I loved it. I found the idea of starting over to be very appealing. After much consideration and reflection, we packed up and moved. I set up shop in an old cow barn and renovated the space into a training area and mini classroom. After busting my ass to get myself into solid financial standing, I went back into debt. I spent a ton of money on equipment and renovations and even took out a loan.

I had a conversation with my great friend Patrick, who I call PJ, and we discussed rebranding the business. In Philly, it was *Inside Out Leadership Training*. PJ, a Marine and Ivy League MBA graduate, suggested "Invictus." I created the logo and rebranded the whole thing under the Invictus name as PJ suggested.

To make a long story short, I took on one client when I got to Minnesota. He then referred me two. Those two referred another two. I had five clients for a while. I called them my "Starting Five" in reference to the fact that they were basketball players. They blew it out of the water. Those five clients referred me many more, and I eventually had a large clientele. I never marketed, referrals only.

Within three years, I was working with athletes primarily on leadership and mindset development. Personal training had gone to the back burner. People were coming to me to work on their head and their heart, with the understanding that their physical performance would improve organically when all aspects of their persona were in alignment. It worked incredibly well.

Of the first fifty clients that I took, every single one of them was elected to or assumed a leadership role. We had multiple guys getting drafted into the pros and even helped an insanely talented, one-of-a-kind personality named Anne achieve her life-long dream—she became an Olympian. Perhaps most impressive was the fact that I had trained five high school teams that went on to state championships in three different sports, all of which were led by captains that were keystone members of the Invictus family.

Now if this all sounds like it was easy, trust me, it wasn't. I made countless, boneheaded mistakes. It was a relentless process of sleepless nights, daily 3:30 a.m. wakeups, financial frugality, and sacrifice, sacrifice, sacrifice and work, work, work. In my first three years of business, I hadn't seen anything or enjoyed any wonders that the great state of Minnesota had to offer. I just worked. In the moments when I wasn't actually working, I was still thinking about work. While my wife and I ate dinner, I asked her for advice about how to foster relationships with clients and parents. Without her support and the trust my clients invested in me, none of it could have ever happened and I wouldn't be here.

Taking Risks

I share the growth and prosperity of the Invictus family because it's essential to understand something that all young men should at the very least consider—taking risks.

Invictus wasn't worthwhile because of the end result. A positive end result is desirable but often fleeting. The everlasting value is found in the process and the journey. Invictus was worthwhile because of the relationships I made and the personal growth that I experienced while building it. Those relationships and growth have carried over into the future. Whatever remaining demons that I had were either dealt with or naturally died off in a direct relationship to the extent of my own personal growth. Shawn, my seventh therapist, was essential in helping me build a methodology and process. The "risk" in my case was investing myself fully in the service of others. The idea of service had soured after my bitter end with the

Army, so I needed to accept the fact that I could still serve others even without a flag on my arm. It was a huge risk for me to bet on myself in a foreign place with people I didn't know while providing a service no one had seen before—mentoring.

Risk can manifest itself in endless ways. It could be something as big as entrepreneurship, military service, and financial investments, or something as seemingly small as trusting those who love you, extending your most authentic self into the world, and expressing emotion.

Regardless of what risk means to you and to what degree it can affect your life, it is not something to be taken lightly. Nor is it an idea to be disregarded. There are certain lessons that can only be accessed through taking risks. The daily squaring up to fear hardens you and thickens your hide. Your tolerance for others' shortcomings increases, and your tolerance for your own weaknesses decreases. Taking *responsible risks* naturally refines and buffers us in the process. We learn how to prepare and build skills that increase our chances of success.

Most importantly, taking risks is inspiring. Every single client that I have ever worked with that busted their ass and took a real crack at greatness inspired me. I sleep well knowing that there are young men and women out there who are willing to get burned in the fight to slay their dragons. These battles and journeys deepen our spirit and enrich our character. They are contagious, and the energy spreads quickly into others, me especially.

Individual risk-taking is a mandatory component of collective human growth. The wisdom learned from individual processes can then be scaled to the masses. I feel strongly that young men must understand that risk-taking is essential to their sense of self-respect and over-all competencies. They also need to understand that they need not do it alone and can embrace the support and kindness that others may extend to them even if it is damaging to their egos. There is no Invictus without my dad, my wife, Gene Miller, Brendan Petersen, Coach A, and slews of people who have helped me along the way.

With that said, don't think (even for one second) that people will do the work for you. Don't think that it is a rainbow ride with puppies and cupcakes. It is work. It is relentless, cold, energy-sucking work *most* of the time, and the learning curve is steep. It is a constant influx of information, and you'll have to learn what to keep and what to discard. The mental challenge is taxing, and the sacrifices you have to make will take your breath away.

If reading about the work, learning, and sacrifice deters you, please lean back in. The self-confidence and competencies that you gain from taking risks are invaluable and will help you excel over the course of your entire life. It doesn't matter if you are afraid. **Fear is acceptable. Cowardice is not.**

The Italian Immigrant

1949–Present

1947 in Frosinone, Italy

There are no roads, electricity, or running water. There are only fields, farmers, and hunters in this small mountain village. The area had been bombed repeatedly during WWII, and many of the houses were damaged from shells and bullet rounds. The village has a one-room schoolhouse which did its best to give the handful of kids an education after they worked in the fields. The land held no opportunity, and the people knew it. Life was bleak. Word had reached them from their paesani who completed the journey to America—the land of opportunity.

Some chose to remain. Others took a risk and left.

A married couple with their three children, two boys and a girl, decided to make the voyage. They packed their meager belongings, boarded a boat, and crossed the Atlantic Ocean. The trip was brutal. None of them had ever seen a boat or an ocean. They got violently seasick. The fear and worry were overwhelming. Their first reprieve was granted upon seeing the Statue of Liberty. Hope found its way into them.

They spoke no English and had Italian names which were un-pronounceable. Customs Americanized each of them by giving them traditional white Anglo-Saxon names, and the schools forced them to learn English. Despite being much older, the children had to repeat grades and start over in kindergarten. They did everything they could to hide their Italian heritage and accents. They were shamed daily by their classmates, teachers, and people in their neighborhood. The other boys in their neighborhood beat the sons often. The kids weren't safe at home with their tyrant of a father either. They had left scarcity in Italy and were met with hostility in America. There was no escape. Life was hard. Many Americans treated them like they were subhumans.

In spite of their trials, tribulations, and harsh treatment from Americans, the kids worked hard to learn the English language and fully dedicated themselves to their schooling. Within years, they had removed any hint of an Italian accent from their spoken English. They excelled in the classroom and generated opportunities for themselves.

One of the sons was given a football scholarship to Villanova University. During his freshman year, he broke his leg and lost his scholarship. He had to work full-time to pay his tuition while attending school. Even though he grieved his loss, he still showed school pride. The negative bias toward Italians continued, and he had to work harder than his classmates. He persevered through the bias and injustice.

He then attended Temple University Dental School where he graduated as the president of his class. He gave the commencement speech in perfect English while his mother was in the crowd listening. That day was the proudest moment in his life.

He went on to have a wonderful career as a dentist

and continues to practice dentistry to this day. There is a tangible love and warmth in the walls of his office. He endured everything from poverty and domestic abuse to social bias, injustice, sacrifice, personal loss, and much more. Even one of those adversities would have stopped anyone, but he persisted and saw himself through all of them.

He epitomizes the American dream and went quite literally from rags to riches in spite of the insurmountable hardships he faced.

That man is my father.

I was raised by a battle-weathered immigrant who knew what it took to make something of yourself, even when the odds were stacked against you. It was a unique upbringing, to say the least. As his only son, I was held to standards far beyond my years and was met with volcanic intensity if I fell short of what he expected of me in terms of behavior.

My dad once saw a bully pick on me at basketball practice. The kid took a swing at me, and I didn't fight back. My dad took me outside into the car and proceeded to scream at the top of his lungs and slam his fists down on the wheel. I sat next to him crying, more upset that he was disappointed in me than from the busted lip left on me by the bully.

"Stop crying. Stop it. What are you? A fucking pussy?"

I was six years old.

Fast-forward three years later and that same bully was punching me again in the cafeteria during lunch at a basketball camp. I didn't want to fight, but he kept at it. Eventually I had enough, and I picked him up and body slammed him, knocking the wind out of him. Then I smashed my fists into his face as many times as I could until his older brother came and broke us up. We were both kicked out of camp for the day, and my dad was called to pick me up.

I sat in the car next to my dad. He was completely silent. I didn't dare cry. I thought for sure that I had disappointed him. I was wrong. He reached over and gently put his massive hand on my forearm. Tears welled up in *his* eyes and we drove home in silence. It was one of the most beautiful moments that my dad and I shared at that time in my life.

Even my buddies knew that "Dr. D" was not someone you messed with. They snapped into shape around him as well, but that didn't mean that we didn't have a blast together. I can't remember a single instance when he said "no" if I asked him to play ball or help me with my homework. Sports were important to my dad, but nothing matched up to his emphasis on excelling in school. So, at thirteen years old when I was in danger of failing out of school, he went berserk. I'll never forget the speech he gave me after he calmed down.

"I'm sorry I yelled. Listen to me, Johnny, there are only two types of people in this world: lions and sheep. You either lead or be led. Nobody can make that decision but you. You need to make that choice right now about what kind of person you want to be. And you need to commit to it for the rest of your life. No excuses. Always take the high road."

He hugged me, kissed me, and told me that he loved me. He told me that he would help me in any way that he could but that I had to do the work, and I did. Not only did I get my act together in school, I also took that speech to heart. By the time I graduated high school, I was an honor roll student and had been awarded every leadership award that our county had to offer, and even was selected for state and national leadership awards as well. I firmly believe that I was given those awards because I watched how my dad treated people. He never wanted *anybody* to fail, and I modeled my leadership style after his example by focusing on helping others succeed.

People thought he was pushing me the whole time, but he had taken his hands off the wheel after we had that conversation at thirteen. I showed him the behaviors he felt were necessary to excel, and he *never* showed me his temper ever again. Today, his stance remains rooted as a loving supporter and observer. In all that time, I have failed many times over. He saw me play a large part in how my life fell apart, but he never interfered. He let me make my own mistakes and calmly told me thousands of times over, "I trust you. You'll figure it out. Keep working. If you need help, ask. Don't quit. Hang tough. I love you." It was quite a departure from how he raised me early on—volcanic temper to loving Zen master.

That's how it was with him. I clued into his fathering style early. He never yelled at me for the heck of it. He never, ever hit me or abused me. His high standards and abrasive rhetoric were always exceeded by his never-ending expressions of peace, love, and support. I was terrified of his temper, but I never felt unsafe around him. I knew that he loved me, wanted the best for me, and was fathering me the best he could. I didn't know why he had a temper the way he did or why he was so tough on me, but I eventually came to understand.

When I was seventeen, my father brought me along to a restaurant to connect with my uncle, my dad's younger brother. Until that dinner, I had never learned anything about my father's father (my grandfather) other than that they didn't have a good relationship. He died well before I was born, so I never met him. When my dad and uncle started to rehash experiences and memories about their father, I couldn't believe what I was hearing. He was an abusive alcoholic whose destructive actions extended far beyond tyranny. He put the whole family through hell, and eventually drank himself to death. To learn all of this was overwhelming. Pieces of the puzzle started to fall into place, and I finally learned why my dad was the way he was and why he raised me the way he did.

It put everything into perspective. He wasn't intense to me whimsically. He raised me from a point of real-life experience. He had to fight to survive his upbringing. He had to fight to survive in America. He never stopped fighting and pushing through adversity. He never caught a break for the first half of his life. By the time I came into the world, all that fighting and struggling had resulted in him crafting a beautiful life for himself, but the memory from his struggles remained. Those memories were charged with energy, which was passed on to me in the form of intensity. Despite the severity of those moments, I always felt loved. He did what he felt he had to do so that his son, a first-generation immigrant, could excel in this country just like he did. He prepared me to handle the worst and promoted me to bring out my best. He felt it was his mission to end the legacy of violence that he experienced and create a legacy of paternal peace and love instead. Even today, I can't imagine the colossal daily effort and self-control that his mission required.

He never took a day off from that mission either. He was always present. I knew that I could talk to him about anything, and that he would meet me where I was at with open arms and genuine, heartfelt affection. He was always willing to share his wisdom and his never-ending love. **My dad always was and will forever remain the strongest, most consistent person in my life.**

A Father's Love

My dad deserves his own story, and you deserve to hear it from him. I can't do it justice, but you can see his influence on me in how I approach life and the challenges it throws at me. I am forever grateful for the focused efforts he made to be the father that he is and all the sacrifices that came with it. Although uncomfortable at times in the early years, his style was effective. He was successful in helping me develop the **behaviors** needed to excel in this country and the **perspectives** necessary to live a beautiful life. I wouldn't change a thing.

With this in mind, it's clear to me that fathers must be permitted to take on their own fathering style when they *choose* to become a father. This includes being tough on their sons when appropriate. With that said, I personally do not condone abuse. It is counterproductive, but I don't judge men who do it. You never know what they have been through themselves. However, I do despise abusive behaviors and the toxic belief systems one has to hold in order to justify abusing one's family. Domestic violence is wrong. These destructive actions can reach into future generations and destroy families. **The fact that my dad never hit me even though he was raised under violence speaks to the caliber of his character and the magnitude of his heart.**

My father made a choice to not pass on the legacy of pain and violence that was placed on his shoulders.

Instead, he made the conscious decision to create a different legacy—one of love, guidance, and support. He was only tough on me when he had to be. His intensity was never whimsical. It was *purposeful* and delivered through a consistent, positive life message. It was obvious to me early on that being a father was something he took very seriously and put a lot of thought into, and it showed.

Becoming a father is a choice, and with that choice comes tremendous responsibility. I have two children of my own, and let me tell you, being a dad is not easy. However, along with that heavy responsibility comes tremendous opportunity. **This is where men can make a profound and positive impact on the lives of their children when they make the choice to become a father, because they can also choose what *kind* of father they want to be.**

I have worked with literally thousands of children and have never met one who is like another. They are all different. This truth should grant men permission to take on the paternal identity they deem necessary to accommodate the uniqueness of their children in order to help them thrive as individuals!

Each father is different, and each child is different. Those differences need to be celebrated and incorporated into a father's love. In doing so, men can become positive role models for their children and help them live beautiful lives while also maintaining their integrity as individuals.

Generational Wealth

I am grateful for the way that my dad raised me. He taught me about what life has in store for all who live on this planet. Sometimes life is hard, life is work, and life is pain. More than anything, he emphasized that **life is beautiful** and packed with meaning when we focus on our health and relationships. He never once mentioned money or wealth as keys to happiness.

Generational wealth is commonly defined as when an older generation passes on its assets to younger generations. Financially, it is considered an advantage. As someone who was in debt, jobless, and completely ignorant to basic personal finance and well versed in the struggles that came along with it, I can affirm that not having money really stinks. I had to learn and master basic financial principles on the fly. Over time, they made a huge difference in the quality of my day-to-day life. Anyone can apply them. Even someone starting at ground zero can learn and change their financial standing (if they're willing to work for it) and eventually aid others in their financial process as well.

Learning basic personal finance is very important. It demystifies and de-villainizes the concept. I now have no issues with money or capitalism whatsoever. They can be incredible forces for good when used responsibly. However, I do take issue with the divinity that people give money and the subsequent behaviors that arise as a result of that devotion. *Money doesn't belong on an altar.*

The most miserable people that I have ever met in my life were hopelessly obsessed with money. They blindly sought out financial wealth, inherited it, or hoarded it without consideration for life's truths. They allowed numbers to consume them and didn't have the perspective necessary to detach from the power of the almighty dollar. The best-case scenario was that they became rich externally but completely bankrupt internally. The worst-case was that they didn't become rich and continued to harbor hate toward everyone, including themselves. Rich or not, these folks are forever *incomplete and resentful* because you can't fill the hole in your heart with cash. It is so sad. If we see "wealth" as strictly related to finance, we're in trouble as a society and will perpetuate broken humans.

Contrary to what many believe, money does not solve everything. It does not create happiness. It does not foster connection. It does not create positive relationships. **Money can buy you a great dog, but only love can make its tail wag.** I can attest to all of that. Money is simply a form of resources. It can be helpful, but if you haven't learned life's lessons, money will backfire on you. **Money is a tool most wisely used to carve out a beautiful life and help elevate the less fortunate.**

With money demoted to a healthier and more functional place, we men can still make a great living, share our resources, and pass on life-related pearls of wisdom to others. Generational wealth then takes on a completely different form. Money is good, but life lessons are the more valuable currency.

True wealth is wisdom.

In order to pass on wisdom, men need to engage themselves in vulnerability. Just as important is how **men lead by example** and exemplify what it means to be a good man and how to live a beautiful life. We can model strong character and virtue and help younger generations understand how to avoid destructive thoughts, emotions, and lifestyles while serving others.

This positive understanding includes but is not limited to the emphasis placed on coherent values like family, love, service, work ethic, faith, and empathy. Just as important are the characteristics of self-discipline, resilience, and grit. If these traits are not consistently at the center of the masculine identity and expressed constructively, we're sunk.

Money doesn't make people better, but wisdom does. **If men prioritize passing on life wisdom to future generations, we can leave it better than we found it.**

Resilient Men

My father is the toughest man that I have ever met. His messaging started very early on, and he modeled what he preached. It didn't matter what I experienced. If I was knocked down by a setback, painful event, or adversity, he would comfort me. Then, he would challenge me with questions.

"Are you going to allow this to stop you?"

"What did you learn from it?"

I heard those questions on repeat for years. Despite the fact that he always extended me emotional support and physical affection, those moments were still hurtful. Understandably so, I was wrapped up in the emotions and pain of whatever I experienced just like anyone else would be. I didn't have the maturity to step outside of it, learn from it, thicken up, and press forward. I was just a kid. I needed him to challenge me.

Fast-forward to now and I appreciate his questions more than ever.

"Are you going to allow this to stop you?"

Allow—to give permission to do something.

No one watches epic adventure movies because they are easy for the protagonist. We watch them because they are great reminders that even the most "average" individual can accomplish extraordinary things when they

123

choose to build an adamant resolve within themselves. **Being resilient is a *choice* made in the face of pain, fear, and adversity.**

Many of the most incredible young men I know are those who at one point were completely terrified and yet made the conscious decision to press forward anyway. When we see someone being resilient, it is inspiring! It calls out the best in us and reminds us that we too can sail through storms.

This point has become a source of frustration for people who understand the value of resilience. Society has overemphasized emotions to the point that emotions have become inhibitors. We focus so much on emotionality, on the feelings we experience in moments of discomfort and pain, that we forget that we can press through them. In fact, it is our moral obligation to ourselves to press through. Otherwise, we become paralyzed by our own emotions.

Resilience cannot be misunderstood or presented as a lack of emotionality. That part of the toxic male message must die off. The reality is that resilience is the vehicle that carries our humanity and our emotions forward. Resilience, in its own poetic way, is one of the most humane traits that a man can have. It is inclusive and validating, not cold and inhumane. Resilience carries all parts of us (especially our emotions) across the finish line, even in the worst of times.

"What did you learn from it?"

I have found that often the knowledge gained from pushing through adversity can be significantly more valuable than inspiration. The reason is that inspiration comes and goes, while the lessons we learn last forever. Inspiration is very important as it may get us back on our feet, but without a learning curve we are doomed to repeat our mistakes. Continuous failure and persistent pain can defeat even the strongest individuals. When men make the same mistakes over and over, they get discouraged or quit. By not learning, they didn't improve. That's why it is vital that we improve our minds while we navigate adversity.

Getting your ass kicked and still stepping up to the plate is definitely a sign of resilience, but we have to be careful about this message. Without being framed properly, it can easily become *false toughness*. Resilience should be constructive. Stepping into adversity needs to build us up. If we interpret resilience as the willingness to get beat just so we can say that we got beat, then that's not resilience. That's stupidity. Resilience is a progress-based virtue. It cannot take us backward. If we go backward willingly, then we become something else entirely—stubborn. Seeking adversity in the hopes that we are labeled as "tough" is not valuable. We need to pursue adversity because of the meaningful value therein, which promotes growth.

Many of the most valuable life lessons can only be accessed through adversity, and in this way, being both *resilient* and a *learner* are paramount to men living beautiful lives.

Work Makes You Happy

Many of the most difficult and complicated conversations I've had with my clients occur after months or even years of the client working their tail off and doing *everything* right, and yet they still *failed*. Or even worse, **they never got an opportunity.** These moments can shatter the toughest of the tough and demotivate the brightest

125

of spirits. It doesn't matter who you are—those moments are hard.

I believe that these moments damage our spirits because somewhere along the line, we were taught to believe that "pulling ourselves up by the bootstraps" would guarantee success. When some learn that's not true, they feel betrayed by the messaging and abandon work altogether.

The truth is that working hard does *not* guarantee success. Nor does working hard promise us an easy life. In reality, work can do the opposite because it can position us to encounter more adversity, more ambiguity, more discomfort, and more heartache. So why work hard? What's the value in it?

First, work *might* provide us with a statistical advantage. Working hard—**the willingness to work, learn, and make sacrifices**—can increase our *chances* to a point that we *may* get an *opportunity* to break through barriers in our lives. Whereas not working hard reduces our chances to zero. **We gain nothing without effort.**

Secondly, and perhaps more importantly, the inherent value of work builds identity. By focusing less on success and failure and more on the skills and perspectives we develop through our efforts, we gain **self-awareness.**

I have worked with many young men who have catastrophically failed in a process they *thought* they should undertake and then harped on the negative result afterward, missing the point altogether. This mindset brought them to a dark place of guilt and self-shaming. Unfortunately, many members of society echo shame from failure.

Work ethic should not be a concept that men use to belittle one another or to justify one's own narrow-minded opinion as to why another man failed or succeeded. In terms of failure and success, there are so many pieces to the puzzle. Social injustice, intolerance, and bias are powerful variables that can make it nearly impossible to succeed. Privilege, wealth, and power can make it nearly impossible to fail. Personal advancement is not as clean-cut as putting out the work or not. Individual circumstances must be taken into account. With this truth in mind, we still **acknowledge results, but we *praise effort*.**

It takes effort to unearth who we are deep down. The benefits of knowing ourselves and embracing our true identities are far more valuable than the fleeting emotions that stem from success and failure.

My dad made this point clear when he was raising me. He literally never taught me to work hard to make more money, get a bigger house, or drive a fancier car. He never spoke of work as a means to a material end or to a place of elevated status. Instead he would emphasize that, "Work teaches you who you are. Work feels good. Work makes you happy."

I believe this message is important for all to hear because masculinity is a journey, not a destination. We express our masculinity differently depending on the season of life we find ourselves in, but we always hold firm to guiding life principles—with *effort* being one of the most important because it promotes us to self-actualize and allows us to feel a sense of contentment with who we have strived to become.

"Treat the Person"

My father has been practicing dentistry for over forty-five years. Aside from him being an excellent father and role model, he's also someone I emulate from a humanitarian perspective.

Many people are terrified of going to the dentist, but not with my dad. His patients come from all over, often flying in from other states. He has patients that are white, Black, Hispanic, Asian, and African. He has patients that are straight, gay, nonbinary, and transgender. I can only shake my head in disbelief when I think of just how diverse his patients are and how he goes above and beyond to make every one of them feel safe in his presence. He tells me all the time, "Johnny, there are a lot of dentists out there. My patients come to see *me*. I never forget that. I believe it's because I don't treat the tooth. **I treat the person.**"

It's a powerful philosophy—one I hope that all men can adopt into their interpersonal habits. It's more than just being empathetic. It's about being a student of each other—to take an active, responsible interest in another's personal history, fears, and wounds—in order to help them feel safe around us.

Sometimes we come across elements of another's personal philosophy that we don't understand, and we armor up to defend ourselves because it makes us uncomfortable. ALOK, a famous Stanford-educated gender non-conforming writer, performer, and media personality, speaks passionately about the dangers of seeking comprehension at the expense of compassion when they advocate for LGBTQ+ rights and anti-violence toward the LGBTQ+ community. "The focus has been on comprehension, not compassion. So people will say, 'I don't understand.' Why do you need to understand me in order to say that I shouldn't be experiencing violence? That's the equation that we really need to interrogate, like what lack of empathy is there in that statement, to just be like, I don't get it? What I don't get becomes a shield for saying, 'I'm okay with you being exposed to violence.' It's never been about comprehension. It's about compassion."

ALOK explains that human compassion must always come first, even if there is disagreement or a lack of comprehension, and I agree wholeheartedly with that philosophy. Many famous intellects have made similar statements regarding the importance of compassion.

But because we often think of ourselves as the main character in life, we can become blind to the plight of others. Albert Einstein said, "Our task must be to free ourselves by widening our circle of compassion to embrace all living creatures and the whole of nature and its beauty." Mahatma Gandhi, Plato, and many other great thinkers have also expressed the importance of decentering ourselves so that we are open to the gifts around us. It's a big world, teeming with life, all of which can benefit from us being willing to step outside of our existence and offer a helping hand.

In mentoring, I build the mentorship based upon where the mentee is in their life, not where I'm at within mine. If I am to be an effective mentor, I need my mentees to know that I don't *judge* them and that they are *safe* when with me. I am there to help them because I care about them, and that needs to always shine through for the mentorship to take root and bear fruit. Sometimes I disagree or am even hurt by my mentees' choices and perspectives, but many people who have helped me also disagreed with my choices and perspectives as well. Yet, they still helped me. Their strength of humanity left me feeling thankful to the point that I want to extend the same level of kindness to others as they showed to me. That's all that matters.

Regardless of personal differences, we can still respect each individual's journey through life by **treating them as a person who is inherently worthy of compassion and respect.**

"Color Me Blue" —Jack Moe

2000–2017

I struggled with depression, severe panic disorder, and post-traumatic stress disorder (PTSD) for over a decade.

It started when I had my first panic attack at sixteen at football practice. I thought I was having a heart attack. The doctors diagnosed me with acid reflux. I was never questioned about whether or not I was experiencing mental distress. The diagnosis put me at ease initially, but over time I suspected that something wasn't right. I had several panic attacks junior year and multiple my senior year. They started escalating in frequency and severity, and I was getting legitimately worried. Despite my concerns, I refused to admit that there might be something wrong. After graduating high school, my panic attacks disappeared while I completed my post-graduate year at Choate Rosemary Hall Prep. Unfortunately, they returned to full strength the summer before I was to attend UPENN as a freshman.

That freshman spring, I had panic attacks weekly. By sophomore year, I had panic attacks daily. I was completely exhausted, getting sick every other week and experiencing a slew of health issues, especially my stomach. Yet, I continued to deny any possibility that I was having mental health issues.

Back then, the stigma around mental health was formidable, and the perception of mental illness was that it was reserved for the guys who couldn't hack it—"pussies" essentially. My eyes opened drastically to the reality of mental illness when a very close friend of mine named Kyle committed suicide. Kyle was an outstanding football player, an academic star, and the most likeable guy you could ever hope to meet. He was superior to me in every way, and I, along with anyone who ever met him, was heartbroken from his passing. He was an incredible human being. The loss was jarring. It made me realize that if it could happen to a guy like him, it could happen to anybody. I deteriorated quickly after finally admitting to myself that I had a problem.

One afternoon I saw an opportunity to sleep, and what was supposed to be a thirty-minute nap turned into a twenty-seven-hour deep sleep. My body essentially quit. I woke up to my buddy Brian knocking on my door.

"Johnny, ready?"

"Bri! Ready for what?"

"It's Wednesday. You coming?"

On Wednesdays, we always got wings at a local restaurant just off campus. It took me a minute to connect the dots and realize that I had been asleep since Tuesday. That was a hard moment. I could no longer carry it silently. I was forced to admit that I was out of my league and decided to go to the campus counselor's office first thing the following morning. It took a few different counselors, but I did eventually link up with a counselor named Dr. Alexander who I felt comfortable communicating with. He had a quiet, nonjudgmental energy and was well versed in helping students navigate issues at home involving substance abuse and addiction.

If not for Dr. Alexander, I'm not sure I would have graduated. Things with my family were just too intense, and I didn't have the skills to handle it. Booze, promiscuity, and self-destruction had become my coping mechanisms. They were ineffective, to say the least. They, along with my belief systems, made the issues and symptoms relentless. Even after Dr. Alexander gave me a strong dose of perspective, I fell hard into the hole of depression after college graduation.

My first bout with depression looked and felt so different than my second. My first run with depression was filled with alcohol abuse and lots of work. I worked my butt off and basically kept to myself. I wore a metaphorical mask that prevented people from seeing how I truly felt, and I didn't have the courage to be honest with myself or the world. Eventually, after the experience described in the "You Have My Attention" chapter, I realized that I hated myself and the person I had become. That's when I dove deep into exploring faith and self-awareness.

Through faith and self-awareness, I basically *learned* my way out of depression. I abstained from sex, laid off the booze, and started to make better lifestyle choices. When it was time for me to join the Army, I was in phenomenal physical shape, and despite the environment at home, I stopped having panic attacks. My issues weren't gone as much as they were pushed down.

But then I got medically discharged from the Army and returned to a broken home where my mother's drug use had intensified. My father had moved out. It was just me and my mother. Those nights were among the worst of my life. Only when I finally left did it all come crashing down.

I fell apart, completely and utterly. Whether you call it a second round of depression or a continuation of the first, it was terrifying. I couldn't have imagined how lonely and unsafe one could feel when depressed. I became so horrified by the thought of being alone that I set many relationships on fire. I subconsciously believed that it was safer to end relationships on my terms than to be hurt by someone else. Rooted in all of that was a paranoia that I was going to be "seen" for what I was, broken and aimless. That was unacceptable, and I felt it was far better to project an image of masculine strength through independence.

Excessive alcohol abuse reentered the picture, because I ignorantly believed that it was the only way I could sleep. Between CITRS, bartending, bouncing, and personal training, I was working four jobs. I had to sleep. I was desperate. Although it seemed that alcohol helped me fall asleep, it didn't help me stay asleep, which made it even worse. I could no longer trust alcohol (or afford it), and luckily a sense of pragmatism won out because otherwise I would have become a full-blown alcoholic.

My job at CITRS allowed me to work with kids in rough areas which was food for the soul and acted as a daily reminder of what is most important in life —health, purpose, relationships, and faith. At times, it got my head above water. It was only after I left CITRS to make more money as a consultant and salesman that I fell back in the hole and stayed there.

The evenings again became nightmarish. I was having night terrors and would wake up completely disoriented, which was then followed by debilitating full body muscle spasms. Getting out of bed in the mornings felt impossible. Happiness, joy, contentment . . . all became things that I felt I didn't deserve. I carried overwhelming shame and guilt. I felt negatively about everything, and my mind threatened the last remaining life principles that I followed.

Despite the shame I felt, I still went through the motions with self-care and did things like daily reading, exercise, and prayer. I didn't feel any positive effects from those habits but did them anyway because all the books I had read made strong cases for them. It was the same with work. I always worked because my dad taught me that if you're willing to work and learn, you're in the game. Looking back, I am now well aware that those habits most likely prevented me from hurting someone, and because of the friend I had lost in college, I never considered hurting myself or committing suicide. But I found myself constantly thinking about quitting on life, disappearing and living out the rest of my days in complete seclusion in nature away from everybody and everything. With each day, the idea of leaving became more and more attractive.

But my appetite to restart working with young men had also been growing. Without the Army or CITRS in my life, I knew that I needed to serve others again. Service had been the only thing that lessened that feeling of drowning, which is exactly what depression felt like. Each day was torture.

For whatever reason, service elevated my mental and emotional state. It got my head above water, took me out of depression and into a more manageable place where I could carve out space in my heart to form a meaningful relationship with a woman who would eventually become my wife.

She supported me 100 percent while I transitioned to become a full-time entrepreneur, and when we moved to

Minnesota, she did the legwork to find me a therapist. We went through quite a few before being referred to Shawn. Unlike other therapists with whom I knew it wasn't going to work, Shawn and I clicked from the moment I walked into his office. I can't explain why specifically, but I imagine that we had individual energies that were remarkably synergistic when open to each other. With him, I was able to learn about myself to the point that whatever I'd kept buried for over ten years came bubbling to the surface. With Shawn's guidance, I entered an insanely difficult and painful recovery phase. Bringing my past to the present was challenging, but I was learning to look at my past through a human lens, and not a masculine one. I became much more motivated to disregard toxic masculine beliefs and engage in constructive behaviors in order to promote my future.

Also, during that time with Shawn, I learned about the bigger picture. As hard as it was to believe the overall state of mental illness in men, my work mentoring young men reaffirmed the reality of the situation. Despite feeling alone in my struggles for years, it became obvious that I was not.

There is a mental health crisis in men, and toxic male ideologies lie at the heart of it.

Toxic Masculinity—A Playbook for Mental Illness

Researchers Wong, Ringo Ho, Wang, and Keino Miller conducted a study in which they analyzed the relationship between men's conformity to masculine norms and their mental health–related outcomes. They summarized the results by saying, "Conformity to masculine norms was more strongly correlated with negative social functioning than with psychological indicators of negative mental health. Conformity to the specific masculine norms of self-reliance, power over women, and playboy-ism were unfavorably, robustly, and consistently related to mental health–related outcomes, whereas conformity to the masculine norm of primacy of work was not significantly related to any mental health–related outcome."

Their findings echoed my own personal experiences as well as the stories that other men shared with me about their own lives. Following toxic masculine ideologies directly prevents men from functioning well in society and negatively impacts their mental health. However, emphasizing the importance of work is okay.

Mental illness is devilish in men because it does not puppet the positive, valuable traits of the male identity like work ethic. It instead preys upon man's code of silence, need for self-reliance, and desire to assert dominance over women and live a playboy lifestyle (drugs, alcohol, promiscuity, etc.). These are all things that men are taught to be and do with the emphatic declaration that they do it independently. It's all a lie. It doesn't make one a "man." It only leads to burnout, isolation, and mental illness.

The truth is that men are built to connect, and much of our health relies on our ability to connect with ourselves, others, and our surroundings. Yet, men are taught to do the opposite—disregard emotion, control others, and achieve dominance. Despite the intensity of these toxic beliefs and the social backlash a man receives when he disregards them, men still cannot accommodate toxic masculinity and foster good mental health. It's crystal clear that "going it alone" has devastating consequences.

In order to prevent and beat mental illness in men, assistance is essential. It's why the subject of "help" was presented in the first chapter. It is a *must*. Without men being vulnerable, expressive, and open to assistance, mental distress does not encounter any pushback.

Mental Health America has stated that men are less likely to seek help for depression, substance abuse, and stressful life events due to social norms, reluctance to talk, and downplaying symptoms. In this way, toxic masculine ideologies are barriers to health and wellness. They serve as **fast tracks to hard stops.** It is for these reasons that mental illness is especially dangerous for men. We are taught to engage in lifestyles that foster mental distress while abiding by codes that magnify its severity. **So not only does toxic masculinity often lead to mental distress in various forms and degrees, the code of silence that men follow allows space for distress to become illness.** Combine that with how men are influenced to quell their distress through behaviors like substance abuse, promiscuity, and withdrawal, and we have a self-promoting crisis.

The stigma that men hold around mental illness is also a magnifier. Contrary to what toxic masculinity suggests, mental illness is not reserved for women or "pussies." **No man, no matter how mentally fit, is exempt from becoming mentally ill.** The stigma is so strong that when men do feel symptoms, they often ignore or deny any possibility that they have a problem that needs to be addressed. Any symptoms related to mental illness not only negatively impact men in and of themselves, but they also carry parasites like guilt and shame, which only take men deeper into isolation. Without assistance, we become our own worst enemy.

Once mental illness in men builds this kind of momentum, it strips us of any possibility to feel happiness, safety, or a sense of belonging. Looking back at my own experience in conjunction with what other men have shared with me, **I marvel at how effective mental illness can be in isolating the men it afflicts.** With toxic male ideologies that preach isolation and the glorification of violence, it is not surprising that suicide in men is much higher than women. According to Mental Health America, the suicide rate for men is four times higher than that of women.

One cannot overstate the wake of destruction that follows suicides. Lives, families, and communities can be destroyed. Each and every one is a tragedy. It is unbearably sad that we have gotten to this point.

The mental health crisis in men is a consequence which stems from illogical behaviors and belief systems.

Believing in and acting through toxic masculine ideologies puts men at a tremendous disadvantage in all aspects of health, especially mental health. They just don't work! Lives are being ruined by following and perpetuating the false, hollow messaging of toxic masculinity. **Only by challenging the traditional toxic male identity** *and* **offering a constructive masculine identity can we right the ship.**

Scarcity versus Abundance

It wasn't that long ago that I was sleeping in my car, dead broke, and jobless with an alcohol problem and severe mental illness. Even now, I still can't believe what has become of my life. If someone told me back then that I would eventually be mentoring young men full-time and

<label>139</label>

happily married with two children, I would have questioned their sanity or assumed they were trying to sell me something.

Luckily, it worked out in ways that I never thought possible, and I became someone with radically different beliefs. My life became beautiful as a result, and I am humbled by and grateful for every person who helped me along the way.

Mentoring has a way of doing that for young men. It can be a transformational human experience. By *"it,"* I mean the relationship between the mentor and mentee.

That relationship is a two-way street by which two people meet in the middle. In order to be a successful mentorship, the *mentee* must be willing to be vulnerable and the *mentor* must be willing to give himself.

In the world of toxic masculinity, competition is a flagship component of being a man. It is a win-at-all-costs mentality, often done purposefully at the expense of others. **Toxic masculinity is centered on me, not we.** It creates this notion that only the individual can win the race.

Mentoring is the archenemy of toxic masculinity because mentors believe there is no such thing as scarcity. James Keller said it best when he explained that "a candle loses nothing by lighting another candle." Mentors live through that truth and are about abundance. We do what we do because we recognize the inherent value in serving others. I can't even count how many times I have referred my mentees to another person. Even though I literally watch money walk out the door of my business, I still know that it's the right thing to do. It allows the mentee to hear another voice and be introduced to another energy. Often, their light grows as a result, and even though

I take a hit monetarily, I gain their trust as someone who genuinely wants to help. Word spreads and *everyone* wins. With abundance incorporated into man's identity, the focus shifts from "how much can I get" to "how much can I give?" Man's competitive nature does not diminish whatsoever. If anything, the drive to compete is magnified through mission-based clarity and altruistic actions. Men fight harder and endure more when in the service of others.

Another crucial value to the abundance mindset is not just how men become willing to help others, but **also how men become willing to help themselves.** The street goes two ways. No side is more important than the other. However reluctant men may be, the first step in the progression to foster positive mental health is that they seek help. They must be willing to walk that road. Only then can they find the energies needed for growth.

My life **began to change** for the better because I asked Mr. and Mrs. C for help, and my life took off as I learned to be vulnerable and open to the energies within this world and within myself.

Toxic masculinity doesn't just inhibit men's ability to be open and connect with others. It also prevents men from connecting with themselves. It is a miserable belief system that takes away energy and closes men off. It naturally creates scarcity and isolation through which men fall deep into mental illness. The abundance mentality allows a man to be vulnerable and grow from internal and external energies while simultaneously giving back along the way. If incorporated into one's identity, the abundance mindset is a belief system that can directly contribute to positive mental health and prosperity in life, especially for men who follow toxic male ideologies.

Forgiveness and Acceptance

Life can be painful sometimes. People hurt us too. Toxic masculinity would have our egos hold on to pain and take an eye for an eye to "defend our manhood." However, holding on to pain causes it to fester and intensify. Instead of managing, processing, and moving past the things that hurt us, the wounds instead become stronger and more painful. By refusing to forgive, our egos bring us into mental illness.

That is why we men have to let go of our hurt and live differently. If we truly want to live beautiful lives, we have to learn how to move on. We have to learn how to forgive. **Forgiveness is liberating.**

Forgiveness is one of those words that people interpret differently. The lack of continuity in understanding forgiveness causes confusion. Men who cannot or refuse to forgive generally lean on one or a combination of three reasons:

1. They have grafted their pain into their identity. They allow it to define them. Without it, who are they? What story about themselves could they possibly tell other than being a victim? The shortcomings in their life are always someone else's fault. There is no personal accountability. It's a diseased, egotistical mindset guaranteed to strengthen a negative cycle.

2. Some men refuse to forgive because they believe that forgiveness does not make them whole. They think the world should pay them back. They don't realize that this perspective lends itself to a life of debt. "I am owed this because I experienced this." It is a miserable belief system. How can anyone live a beautiful life if they are constantly keeping score?

3. Men believe that they don't deserve forgiveness. They just can't see it. They believe their pain is earned and should remain with them. They become possessive because the pain is theirs. It's a parasitic mentality that feeds on its believer. This belief causes blindness to the inherent opportunity in every day to carve out a beautiful life. It takes the sense of personal accountability overboard and prevents men from seeking light in their lives because they believe they belong in the dark. The feelings of shame are overwhelming and make men believe that they must never feel happiness. Mental illness thrives on this mentality because false feelings can get intertwined with truth. They're difficult to separate and often swim in waters with other ideas like honor and duty. For many men, especially service members, it makes forgiveness seem ridiculous and a beautiful life unattainable. Untangling that web takes time, a dedication to learning, and a ton of support from others who speak that language. But it is possible.

Forgiveness is the ability to live a beautiful life in spite of all failure, shortcoming, and pain. That's it. Let's not complicate it past that. Forgiveness is simply the ability to relieve ourselves of debt and carry on toward something meaningful.

Another crucial ability that men must have to live a beautiful life is the ability to practice acceptance. Like life and people, our personal circumstances can hurt us too. Acceptance allows us to fully acknowledge a situation for what it is.

Without acceptance, we will self-victimize and lose sight of the truth. **We dwell on what things should be and how they hurt us, instead of what they are and how they could help us.** Often when men refuse to accept the actuality of a tough situation, they will obsess and allow their energies to become monopolized by negativity. Their mindset then becomes oriented to the details of problems they are experiencing, which only digs a deeper hole. If we silence our hurt egos and accept a situation for what it is while redirecting our energies toward becoming solution-oriented, then we have a shot at growing through adversity. We can also just practice acceptance and move on. Either approach allows men to ground themselves in reality and accept things for what they are, or accept the responsibility to try and change them. With either method, acceptance still allows good to find its way into our lives, while dwelling, denial, and self-victimization only hoard the bad.

True forgiveness and acceptance allow us to rise above it all and lift others up along the way, which sometimes includes our transgressors and even ourselves. Forgiveness and acceptance are expressions of strength, not weakness. They are strengths that promote positive mental health and position men to live beautiful lives.

People in the Waiting Room

Before I was referred to Shawn, the therapist asked me if I had any problems with Shawn being gay. I had played sports with gay teammates, served in the Army with gay soldiers, and had gay friends. My reply was, "No. No problem at all." During our first session, I gave him a high-level summary of why I was there, and he took it all in. It was an intense experience for both of us. Afterward I said, "I can't carry all this shit with me anymore. I'm willing to do the work, and I hope you can help." With that he smiled, and we scheduled far out in advance.

I saw Shawn every week for years. I never missed a session or was late. Time with him in his office was *that* valuable to me. His waiting room also proved to be a valuable learning ground. I was always early which allowed me to sit across from others waiting for services. Many different people came to work with him: straight, gay, transgender, nonbinary, and gender nonconforming. I never pried for specifics about his patients, but I did ask him how many other patients he had who struggled with toxic masculine ideologies.

"More than you think," he said.

"More men?"

"No, more everyone. It hurts everyone."

That was a humbling realization for me. For years, I thought it was just me. Then I mentored, and I thought it was just men. Then I learned that **toxic masculinity affects** *everyone.*

I went to Shawn for help. Some can't.

I had a car to get me to and from his office. Some don't.

I was able to afford medical services. Some can't.

I had several mentors guiding me. Some don't.

I had a relationship with Marissa who was willing to challenge me. She didn't have to.

I didn't have to be constantly aware of the danger of being violently victimized or discriminated against. LGBTQ+ people do.

I don't face systematic oppression. Some people do.

Toxic masculinity affects everyone, but not everyone has the same support, access to care, resources, or social standing. I'm not for creating a hierarchy of pain, but I do feel that men need to acknowledge that toxic masculinity impacts people differently and that the path to mental health is going to look different for everyone, and in many cases, is incongruously more difficult for some people because of societal factors.

Ruth White, a professor in the USC Suzanne Dworak-Peck School of Social Work, states that, "In black communities, reluctance to seek both physical and mental health care can often be attributed to a general distrust of the medical establishment. This distrust is not without merit: black communities have been exploited by the U.S. government and medical community in the name of medical advancement. Much of the pushback against seeking treatment also stems from ideas along the lines of: We have survived so much adversity and now someone is going to say that there's something wrong with us. In addition to shifting the cultural narratives surrounding mental health, the practical considerations of cost and access to care must be considered. Today, there is a critical shortage of practitioners that disproportionately affects people of color, while prohibitive insurance and health care costs often make it more challenging for low-income individuals to access needed treatment. This has an outsize impact on African Americans, who have among the lowest rates of health care insurance of any ethnic group."

The point is that while toxic masculinity affects everyone, the roads in and out of mental illness will always be different. These differences have to be acknowledged and respected and in some cases, may require us to offer assistance to those in need even while we seek help ourselves.

Humanize Men for Mental Health

There are many campaigns and slogans designed to re-duce the stigma around mental illness in men. "It's okay not to be okay" sticks out to me. It's true; it's okay not to be okay. But it's only okay to not be okay if you're a *person*, **not if you're a** *man*. Toxic masculinity forces the idea that a man must always be autonomous and good to go. Yet somehow, it's widely understood that it's normal for people to have problems.

In order for men to take those first difficult steps through the gateway into a process and progression to-ward mental health, we must establish a truthful hier-archy of the masculine identity that allows men to ac-knowledge that they are **people first, men second.** By humanizing men, the lone ranger message will no longer hold water and the stigma surrounding mental illness in men will dissipate naturally.

When I first moved in with Mr. and Mrs. C after finally saying goodbye to my mother, Mrs. C made a point to re-mind me of my humanity. **"I know you're a big, strong man JohnnyD, but you're a person too. And people need help sometimes."** All these years later, it's never been more relevant.

By acknowledging that men are people first—and people sometimes need help—we allow space for men to take the first steps to seek and accept support.

The Faceless Woman

2019

It's easy to skid out when the snow fall is this heavy. He still turns on his blinker even though no one else is on the road. While turning right, the rear tires slide into the opposite lane, and he narrowly misses the mailboxes across the street. He exhales and shakes his head.

Even with four-wheel drive, he's not confident that he'll make it up the hill. The wheels are spinning out on flat ground. He shifts into low gear, looks for an area for his wheels to grab, and steadily climbs the hill. He has the heat blasting, but the windshield still fogs up. He wipes it with his gloved hand.

"I can't see shit," he mutters to himself.

As he gets to the top of the hill, there is a silhouette just ahead. He sees a person walking on the side of the road who suddenly steps into the middle of his lane causing him to stomp on the brake. He hears the tires groan over the snow and his car skids out, spinning him until he is horizontal across both lanes.

He worries that he hit the person but is relieved to see the figure still walking, eventually disappearing into the dense snow. He takes several deep breaths.

He reverses, turns the wheel, drives forward, reverses again, and then repeats until he is back in his lane facing the right direction. Aware that the person is ahead of him but unable to see, he drives very slowly with his eyes peering over the dashboard and hands white-knuckling the wheel. The dark figure comes back into view, and he places his foot onto the brake while carefully steering into the lane alongside the stranger.

As he rolls down the passenger side window, he notices it's a woman. The cold air hits him. It is bitter and biting. She must be freezing, he thinks to himself.

"Need a ride?"

Her hands are in her pockets and her chin tucked down into her red scarf, which is barely visible above her black coat collar. Her black wool hat sits just above her eyes, and her scarf is up over her nose. He can see the snow sticking to her eyelashes and air freezing on the front of the scarf over her mouth.

The woman doesn't look at him. She just keeps walking.

"Do you want a ride?"

Annoyed that he had to ask twice, the words leave his mouth on gravel. Without warning, she turns toward his car, and he has to stomp on the brake again. The car spins out, and he does everything he can to not sideswipe her. The window is still open, and snow falls onto the passenger seat.

He's outraged at her carelessness. She opens the door, gets in, and sits on the snow. She pulls the door shut, remains motionless, and doesn't put on her seatbelt or say a word. She's hunched over with her eyes fixed on the floor.

He is irate to the point of speechlessness. He stares at her. She doesn't close the window. She doesn't look at him. He can see her breath escaping through her red scarf and then being pulled out the window by the wind. He closes the window, and they sit there in silence for what seems like forever.

Even with the heat on, he can feel the cold air falling off her. He hates the sound of her breathing, so he turns on the radio. He lightly presses down on the gas pedal, and the car inches forward.

"Where are you going?"

No response. He regrets offering her a ride and resents her for accepting it.

"I'll take you to the bus station down the road. That work for you?"

She reaches forward and turns off his radio. He turns it back on immediately.

He barks out, "What is your fucking problem?"

She puts her hand back in her pocket and just stares at the floor. He's about to lose his patience and pulls into an empty parking lot. He takes a deep breath and fires out.

"Look. You're supposed to walk against traffic. You were walking on the wrong side of the road, dressed in all black. I nearly hit you. Twice."

He steadies himself, "You need to be careful."

She turns away from him and looks out the window. He softens his tone.

"Please understand. I'm trying to help you. The roads are ice."

He extends himself and lightly puts his hand on her left arm, but she pulls it away. A black, bubbling hatred erupts within him. He punches the radio off and pulls out of the parking lot, and they spend the rest of the ride in silence.

He stops at the bus stop.

She exits quickly, slams the door shut, and walks to her right.

He puts his blinker on and listens to it click for a while. Then he turns left.

Angry Men

I wrote this story many years ago after I nearly hit a female pedestrian during a no visibility snowstorm. She walked on the wrong side of the road and then crossed without looking. I missed her by a few feet. It all happened in a blink of an eye.

I was furious and vocalized a horrible, tar-filled comment related to her womanhood. I heard the words leave my mouth and couldn't believe that those thoughts existed in my head. Even at my worst, I had never said anything remotely similar or even thought about any woman like that.

I hated hearing those words and was disappointed in myself for saying them. **I knew that I didn't feel that way about women.** I had to reflect: Why were those words in my brain at all? Where did they come from? Why was I so quick to jump to anger and disgust?

I had nothing against her and genuinely wanted to help.

Many memories came back to me the more I thought about it. I had heard men talk about women like that my entire life. Their comments always confused me and made me uncomfortable. They modeled otherwise virtuous behaviors. I liked some of those men. In fact, I even admired a handful of them. It created conflict within me.

I have always believed and still continue to believe that men are defined by their actions. However, as I've gotten more life experiences under my belt, I have realized that words also hold tremendous power. The way many men talk about women is saturated with conviction to the point that even the most ridiculously ignorant comments can carve out space in our brains. You may parrot what you've heard other men say when your emotions are high

151

or your guard is down. You may not mean those words when you say them. Yet somehow, they stayed in you and eventually echoed out of your mouth.

Men are indoctrinated to limit our emotions. Anger and disgust are deemed acceptable, but sadness, loneliness, and even happiness are not. Many men fear expressing emotion because of emotional policing. Men shame other men by calling them a pussy or a bitch. If you want to shame a man, feminize him. This insult hits hard because it derives from completely false toxic masculine belief systems: Women are weak. Women are fragile. Women need our help. Women are emotional. These lies preach the blind intolerance, fragilization, and judgment of women and imply that women need men's help. To complicate that, women show emotions. Emotions are threatening to men, which means women are threatening to men.

Put the two together and we have a collective toxic male belief that women are weak and need our help, and women are emotional and are therefore threatening, worthy of our hate. **This creates a terrible dichotomy in which men feel forced to hate and protect women simultaneously.**

In fact, both beliefs are completely unfounded. Yes, men are taught to simultaneously hate and protect women, but **it's not about women.** It's about the attribute—expressing emotion. Emotions are a natural part of life. So really, when men are intolerant of women's emotions, it's really a displaced intolerance of themselves.

Life often throws experiences at us that drum up more than one emotion, but toxic male ideologies would have *all* of men's emotions funneled through a narrow opening: anger. In those moments, emotions, which should otherwise be multifaceted and embraced, are instead pressurized, hardened, and concentrated. Their intensity is then expressed aggressively. Dr. Raymond DiGiuseppe, PhD and chair of the psychology department at St. John's University, conducted research that showed men and women experience relatively similar levels of anger, but they differed in *how* they experienced it. Specifically, men expressed anger aggressively and compulsively. This makes sense because aggression is celebrated as manly in toxic male culture. The combination of emotional suppression, acceptance of anger, and praise for aggression creates space for men's negative emotional habits to be normalized and socially accepted, even though they're destructive.

However, anger is an acceptable human emotion, and it has a place in the human experience. It can actually be quite helpful when expressed responsibly. But men are not given the space as boys, teenagers, and young men to learn to express other emotions. A situation which would normally trigger sadness leads to anger for men. It's what we're taught to do, and we are shamed ruthlessly by other men when we fail. Unfortunately, many women shame men for showing other emotions too. It is a widely accepted cultural belief that men should not cry, and the social degradation that accompanies male emotional expression is well practiced. As boys, we learn to keep our emotions hidden, buried, and ignored unless we want to be seen as weak in the eyes of others. This practice improves as we enter adulthood and can become a point of pride. Men then become incredibly intolerant of people's emotions not only because they're taught to do so, but also because it allows them to paint themselves as superior to "emotional people."

153

That man in my story felt many emotions, not the least of which was relief and genuine concern for the faceless woman. He wanted to help her but expressed himself to her through escalating verbal aggression. What is a woman supposed to do when a man expresses himself like that? She didn't say a word or change her energy. She stayed silent, yet the man still fell over the edge. Her waters were calm and his were boiling.

It's not about women. It's about men and how anger festers within us because we don't know how to express it constructively.

Emotions make people human. They do not make them weak, nor does emotional suppression make one strong. Those who practice a broader emotional spectrum engage in life in more enriching ways. It allows them to connect more readily with others. This doesn't mean that men should emote like women. It just means that men should learn how to emote. Emotions are natural. They make us human. There is a tremendous freedom granted to those who are willing to embrace all their emotions and express them freely. If men continue to limit their self-awareness and deny themselves the freedom to express themselves fully, there will always be intolerance and destructive hatred toward those who show emotion and toward humanity in general.

Vulnerability

Anger can be acceptable, useful, and positive. It is not an emotion that should be ignored. It needs to be processed and expressed constructively, just like other emotions. However, men believe it to be a symbol of strength, and that's when anger becomes the most destructive emotion that men can have. It denies men access to other emotions. **Toxic male ideologies do not allow men to be vulnerable or accept the vulnerability of others.** The male interpretation of vulnerability is warped and makes men feel threatened:

- They imagine floodgates opening and all emotions pouring out.

- They imagine people being played by their own heartstrings.

- They see critical thinking go out the window and emotions taking control of the ship.

- They see emotional people as those who are not in control of themselves.

- They see expression as weakness.

- They see vulnerability as a surefire way to be taken advantage of.

Men catastrophize vulnerability.

Brené Brown, famous researcher and storyteller, discusses vulnerability at great length. I think all men should watch her TED Talk, "The Power of Vulnerability," and read her book *Daring Greatly* even if only to broaden their understanding of vulnerability. If learning from her was like getting tackled in football, her perspective would be the equivalent of getting the snot knocked out of you. Men believe that getting hit that hard is good for a young man. It toughens them up. And in that way, so is learning about Brown's philosophy. It knocks you flat.

Brown said, "Vulnerability is not winning or losing; it's

having the courage to show up and be seen when we have no control over the outcome. Vulnerability is not weakness; it's our greatest measure of courage." This new way to look at strength challenged my thinking and made me question my loyalty. Am I most faithful to being strong and courageous or to being closed and angry? Which is the truer form of masculinity?

For me, the answer was obvious. I want to be strong and courageous. I want those virtues to be expressed in constructive ways—in ways that build up my "self," my relationships, and my life. Being closed threw me into a decade-long decline. It didn't work and I was miserable.

My realization encouraged me to interact with women in new ways. I noticed that I started recognizing traits in them that I had been blind to for years. Over time, my appreciation for gender differences grew but was surpassed by a sincere appreciation for women's sense of humanity. **I grew to admire their strength as human beings far more than their femininity.** I found their capacity for empathy most attractive. In my line of work as a mentor for young men, empathy is essential for success. In order to be empathetic, I had to be vulnerable. Vulnerability is the opposite of what I was taught about being a man.

Ironically, learning vulnerability didn't make me less of a man. It made me stronger as a person, and increased my capacity to execute the masculine principles that I found to be constructive and helpful.

It started by embracing all my emotions and having the spine to express them when appropriate. It was messy at first, as it is anytime you learn a new skill. I made lots of mistakes and shared parts of myself with people that I shouldn't have. It was difficult and at times ugly. Over time, my self-awareness and ability to self-express improved. I was able to connect with people differently, especially women.

When men are vulnerable, they find new sources of strength because they no longer keep their energies closed. They become open, and new energies find their way in. When closed, energies stagnate. When open, growth occurs in abundance. **With growth comes strength.**

If you as a reader need permission to explore your emotions, you have permission. Dive into and explore your emotionality. Be angry if you need to, but don't *just* be angry. Explore the whole spectrum. Learn to freely express your emotions in ways that are responsible and constructive. A friend, mentor, confidant, therapist, family member, movement, the arts, and reading are all good mediums to learn self-expression. It is the most worthwhile journey that you'll ever undertake—**lose your false self to find your true self.**

Life looks so different when we know who we are, accept our emotions, and practice vulnerability with ourselves and others. With these elements in place, **light has a way of finding men and making them stronger than ever before.** Then there is no need to hide any part of ourselves or spew our hurt onto others, especially women. You can be who you are without apology or explanation. You earn the freedom to walk your own path.

Relationships with Women

Vulnerability shifted my perspective and allowed me to build wonderful relationships with women based on their humanity and spirituality. By connecting with women in this way, I changed. Many of my belief systems unraveled from there and could no longer hold water. By following the age-old golden ratio of two ears, one mouth (*listen twice as much as you speak*), I learned so much about life by listening to how women experience it.

Women have always experienced and continue to experience tremendous bias, hardship, and suffering, the majority of which has been placed upon them by men. Listening to their stories, without interference from my indoctrinated masculine perspectives, painted an incredible picture that allowed me to freely acknowledge their profound resilience, intelligence, and humanity in spite of the adversity they face.

Think about it.

Half the planet is made up of women. If you exclusively consider life through a male perspective, you're only reading half of the global story. You're operating with an incomplete data set, and what you have isn't good enough. We men must consider the female experience in order to grow past our masculine inhibitors.

While at CITRS, I worked under a woman named Jeanne, a positive psychologist and strengths development expert. She is an excellent human being in every way—compassionate, brilliant, intuitive, creative, and patient. You can talk to her about *anything*, and she has the grace to field it. Just being around her made me want to be a better person, and I always had questions. We were having a discussion, and I admitted that I wasn't sure how to engage women in certain situations. She offered me her insight, "It may be a good approach for you to treat all women as you'd want your daughter to be treated."

I am sure that I must have been staring at her with an odd look on my face because she repeated herself to make sure that I heard her correctly, but I heard her perfectly the first time. I was replaying thousands of past interactions with women in my head while applying this new standard to those moments. I fell miserably short. I had never realized that I always subconsciously intended to treat my daughter differently. It was a lot to process. First, I told Jeanne thank you. She didn't owe me that insight, and it could have been uncomfortable for her to work as a woman in an otherwise all male office. I found her strength to be humbling. Over time, I put a lot of thought into her suggestion and my hypothetical daughter.

How did I intend to treat my daughter?

I imagined that I would treat her as a unique human being and respect her hopes, dreams, and inherent value. I would support her growth process. Most importantly, I would hope that she *always* feels safe and loved around me.

Although not perfect, it was quite a departure from my thought processes prior to Jeanne's suggestion. Abundant beauty entered into my life as a result of this mindset and approach. My initial gateway to a new relationship with women was a "daughter standard," but the nature of the gateway is inconsequential compared to the growth men can achieve as a result. It is a much more functional way to interact with women on a daily basis. I still have my blind spots that pop up every once in a while. I listen to them and lean them against the standards that have evolved since that conversation with Jeanne. This approach has allowed tremendous admiration for women to enter my heart, and much of the inherited anger that society injected into me has subsided.

With that loss of anger came opportunity for happiness. I was able to build a one-of-a-kind relationship with a very special individual who eventually became my wife and the mother of my children. In spite of all the damage from my mother, my wife managed to circumvent that baggage and strike the center of me. Among other things, she became my closest confidant and most trusted advisor. It is mainly because of our relationship that I have learned to extend trust to women in general. By reopening that bridge, I have discovered wonderful friendships with women and partnerships with women advisors, all of whom are trustworthy and insightful and challenge me to grow. I'm thankful for all of them, and I express gratitude toward them regularly.

It should surprise no one that every aspect of "me" (professionally, financially, health-related, etc.) has taken off as a result. Tremendous light has entered my life as a result of these relationships, and my wife is at the heart of it. It wasn't easy, but things worth doing rarely are. **By no longer carrying hate in my heart, I was able to harmonize with women and in turn, myself.**

Evolution of the Daughter Standard

Jeanne's gift to me of the "daughter standard" first came to fruition because I knew I needed to harmonize with women. Eventually the standard was applied to everyone, not just women. The driving growth force behind that expansion was love. I hoped to love my daughter and help her thrive. What stopped me from applying that same notion to other people? At that time in my life, it wasn't easy for me to love someone if I didn't know them. Social scientists sometimes refer to this as "contact hypothesis," which is the theory that intergroup contact under appropriate circumstances can reduce prejudice. Thinking on my internal gap, it didn't take me long to see that I didn't have to meet someone to love them, nor did I have to withhold love for anyone if I was willing to look at love in different contexts.

Clinical psychology research has identified two types of love: passionate and attachment. The Greeks had words for many different types of love: Eros (sexual passion), Philia (deep friendship), Ludus (playful love), Agape (love for everyone), Pragma (long-standing love), Philautia (love of the self), Storge (family love), and Mania (obsessive love). These examples prove a point—there are many different types of love.

For me, "love" became more dynamic. I love my wife but not the same way I love the homeless person on the corner. I love my buddies but not the same way I love my business partners. However, there is a commonality in the undercurrent of how I express love toward others, and it's centered on the idea that I hope for everyone's *ultimate good*, regardless of whether I know them or not. Meaning, I want people to live good lives and will help them along if they allow me.

I'm far from perfect and am still learning how to bring this concept to the front of my daily life and interpersonal habits, but it's already made a meaningful difference. I'm no longer angry at people, nor do I feel at odds with others as toxic masculinity would have me be.

In this way, "love" is *not* a sentiment that men must reserve for those they know. **Love can also be energy that men put into the world, which contains an earnest desire for *everyone* to live freely as their true selves and to grow within the human experience.**

Helping men understand that they are permitted to love others and teaching them how to bring love into their daily lives requires deconstructing toxic masculinity's legacy of anger and emotional suppression and building up self-awareness and emotional intelligence.

Commit to Calm

Deconstructing men's legacy of anger is difficult. It requires men to **commit to being calm.** One of the most challenging aspects within that process is learning how to be calm while still processing and expressing emotion. It's not easy. We can't pursue calmness at the cost of losing emotion entirely. Without emotion, the best moments in life are just like any other. Without emotion, life is cold. We cannot allow ourselves to become *indifferent*.

No matter their intensity, our feelings are temporary, fleeting, and reactive to our surroundings. If we're all emotion, we lose sight of the bigger picture. That is a recipe for *regret* because it *feels right* in the moment, but we forget about all the other factors at play and the people our decision may impact. Then we have to hustle to make up the ground lost from our poor decisions.

The key is to harmonize our heads with our hearts by pairing critical thinking with emotional intelligence.

In terms of making decisions, emotions are advisors, and it is wise to listen to them. They deserve to be acknowledged and validated, but we can only make decisions *with* them. Emotions can never be behind the wheel. **Emotions are terrible problem solvers and awful decision makers.** They have no loyalty to guiding life principles. As such, emotions do not have a true north. There is no way to maintain bearing. After we make an errant, emotional decision at a critical moment, we are left wondering, "What the hell was I thinking?"

Toxic masculinity allows men to operate reactively. Even after poor decisions, the toxic male ego will find a way to justify negative actions. In these instances, actions happen without awareness of one's true self, and the post-action processing is run without an authentic conscience. **With toxic masculinity at the helm, there is little opportunity for self-awareness and self-regulation through which a man can accept all his emotions non-judgmentally, and thereby retain control of himself in order to make good decisions.**

Learning self-awareness and self-regulation are essential processes in order for men to mature emotionally.

We can't be raging volcanoes all the time. It's too destructive.

We can't be emotionally volatile all the time. It's too limiting.

We can't be offended all the time. It's too hurtful.

Destructive, limited, and hurt are words that I would use to identify the side effects of toxic male emotional ideologies which preach limiting our emotional spectrum to anger and disgust. **It causes men to have big expectations with thin skin.** It's a horrid combination. Men have to build the skills needed to become emotionally intelligent so that they experience the exact opposite effects. Men need to be constructive, growth-oriented, and resilient.

Committing to calm allows us to make fully present, conscious decisions that take all elements of ourselves, our experience, and others into account. It's how we win championships in spite of tremendous adversity, doubts, and naysayers. We don't allow our emotions to get caught up in any of that. We stay centered within ourselves.

Committing to calm is not a rejection of emotion or

a façade that lies and says, "I'm okay," when you're not. Instead, it is an active acceptance of all our emotions. It's how we make progress during hard times by preventing self-sabotage. Committing to calm is also how we retain the ability to enjoy life when times are good. We can still feel the enormously valuable emotions like satisfaction, happiness, and contentment, but we don't allow those positive emotions to derail us either. Several of my most reckless, numbskull decisions in my life were made when I was having a great time with my buddies. It's not solely negative emotions that can lead to poor decisions. Positive emotions can be just as destructive if we aren't present.

If we truly want to redefine masculinity, there is no better place to start than self-awareness and self-mastery. We have to make peace with our emotions in order to make peace within ourselves.

A Wretch's Music

2019

Years ago, when I first started going into empty churches, I was overwhelmed by the noise in my head. Only after years of practice did my thoughts dim and the serenity of prayer gain traction.

On sunny days, light shines through stained glass windows and caresses the wooden pews with mellow, warm colors. It is so quiet that I can hear my footsteps, my breath, and even my heartbeat. I find the silence to be healing and its clarity illuminating.

This day's visit was during a rainstorm. There was no sunlight or warmth. The church was dark, cold, and damp with a faint smell of mildew from the carpets by the doors. Despite the lack of light, I saw a figure out of the corner of my eye enter through the door. It was a strange man with a shaved head in a sleeveless shirt. He was covered in tattoos. He struggled to breathe and moved with visibly painful arthritis. I am sure that I would have heard his bones popping if not for his deafening wheezing. He looked like a man with a rough past.

He didn't notice me even after I lit a candle and sat down in a pew across the altar from him. I don't think he could hear anything over his wheezing or see me in the shadows. He walked carelessly toward a pew and tripped on a drum set. After he regained his balance, he tried to silence the symbol which continued to sound throughout the church. Everything about him overwhelmed the peaceful silence I sought in prayer.

He turned back to the exit and opened the door. The rain was coming down hard and sounded like a waterfall. Instead of leaving, he sat down in the choir, grabbed a guitar, and placed it across his lap. He plucked the strings while he tuned it. It was loud and unpleasant.

After he adjusted the strings, he cleared his tobacco-tarred throat and began to play. It was unlike any sound I had ever heard before. His music was beautiful, eloquent, and effortless, which contradicted the sight of his broken body.

The music he made filled me with great emotion. After a few chords, I decided that I should leave. I felt that his music was not meant for human ears, and that I should bow out as quietly as possible so as to not disturb his concert.

I bent over and shuffled out of the pew silently and walked past the candle that I had just lit. The weather outside was howling, but the air inside the church was still, so still that the candle moved with me as I walked by. Remaining in the shadows, I was able to exit the church without disruption.

I got in my car, turned on the ignition, and took several breaths to try and process what I just saw and heard. I didn't come up with any answers. Instead, I felt gratitude.

As I drove away, I saw his large Harley-Davidson motorcycle with an out of state license plate parked under the overhang of the church. It had a bumper sticker on it, "For Whom the Bell Tolls."

The Power of Prayer

Anyone who knows me knows that I rarely, if ever, talk about my faith. It is intensely private and not something that belongs to anyone else. However, the practice of prayer is not meant to be kept confidential.

After years of study and practice, I have learned that the power of prayer cannot be overstated. It allows us to transcend the broken human condition and enter into a space filled with energy that transcends our earthly existence.

It sounds spacey and corny and maybe it is. But feet to the fire, I believe it. I think that everyone should practice prayer, which is decidedly different than reflection. **When we reflect, we ruminate on human principles. When we pray, we contemplate spiritual principles.** Both are important, but prayer connects us to something bigger than us.

Prayer can become a *true north* guiding force in our lives when aligned to guiding spiritual principles. I am not nearly as concerned with what people believe in, as much as I am hopeful that they believe in *something*. Ideally, that something is structured in a way that promotes the individual to become a peaceful, loving, hard-working, and resilient person. In order to actualize those benevolent concepts, we all can pray upon them and how our thoughts, feelings, and actions align to them, if at all.

Prayer does that for us. It is a way of leaning who we are against **the person we are meant to become. Prayer facilitates that alignment.**

That beat-up old man challenged me to be the person *I am called to be*. I could have gotten upset at him for destroying the silence I needed. However, by that point in my life,

I had learned to accept people as they are. It allowed me to be a nonjudgmental observer, and I am convinced that is the reason I was blessed with the opportunity to listen to his music. **He went to the church to seek shelter from the rain, and I went to seek shelter from myself.** It was a moment that I will never forget. I won't remember how his music sounded, but I will always remember how it made me feel. If nothing else, it was a reminder to pray for humility and gratitude, and to love people for who they are and who they could become, not what they look like. In that moment, his music and my prayer allowed beauty to enter both of us. We were two people with nothing in common, and yet we still *connected*.

That is the power of prayer.

"I'll Meet You at the Lake"

2021

It was Wednesday and I got a text out of nowhere from a young man that I had mentored for years. I was so excited to see his name pop up on my phone because I hadn't seen or heard from him in a while, despite having reached out to him several times. I opened my phone and read his text.

"Hey coach, can you talk?"

Although I had suspected that he was having a hard time, my heart still dropped.

"Yes I can talk. On phone or in person?"

"In person if you can."

"Does Friday at 12 work?"

"Can you talk today?"

"Yes. When works for you?"

"Now if you can."

"I'll meet you at the lake."

Minnesota has over ten thousand lakes. They're everywhere and each one is stunning. For this meeting, we chose to link up at Lake Minnetonka. Before leaving, I gave my wife and kids a kiss and told them I loved them. Then I grabbed my keys, wallet, and phone, hopped in my car, and headed out with the windows down. It was a picture perfect 72-degree day with a slight breeze and not a cloud in the sky. I parked near a Caribou Coffee shop, sat down on a bench overlooking the lake, and waited for him, wondering what his deal was.

When I saw him, he looked physically fit and a little older than the last time I saw him. He saw me, and the big smile stretched across his face along with his body language put me at ease. He was fine. He just needed to talk. We slapped hands, hugged, and then sat down on the bench.

The first thing out of his mouth was an apology for not responding to me, which I quickly accepted while reassuring him that he didn't have to apologize. The following thirty minutes were spent with him describing his personal experiences over the course of the past eighteen months. I could not believe my ears. This twenty-year-old kid had gone through the wringer with real-deal life issues—everything from family and health to school and depression. It was one thing after another.

After he was done, I said, "Thank you for sharing that with me."

I took a breath, paused and then said, "I gotta be honest. That's a lot to digest."

He burst out laughing and said, "Yeah. Yeah, it really is."

"Going through all of that . . . I imagine that it left a mark or two."

"Oh yeah, I'm not the same person anymore."

And from that statement, we launched into a long discussion about pain, personal growth, and identity. Adversity had given him the opportunity to explore his identity. He found himself, his *true* self, and was no longer interested in aligning himself to societal expectations of who people thought he should be. Despite the sadness in his past, it was a beautiful conversation full of redemption and hope, all enjoyed with a gorgeous lake view with dozens of sailboats in the distance. When we were done, I reminded him that there is no need to go through things alone and encouraged him to contact me at any time. I told him how I felt about him, we hugged, and we went about our days.

Later that night, after my wife and I ate dinner and had put the kids to sleep, I checked my phone. I saw that he had sent me a text.

"Thank you for today coach. I will for sure call you more. Let's meet up again when I get back from school. Love you and your family."

Mentors of Men

I have had countless conversations with young men just like that one, and they never get old. Each one is powerful and completely unique, and I feel blessed to have the opportunity to serve them and promote their individual journey. As mentors, we are called upon to aid young men in finding and walking the path that belongs to *them*. **There is no one way to be a man.**

I know this to be true because of the differences in the men that took me under their wings, stood alongside me, and helped guide me on my way. They are all so different from one another, not just in race, religion, and orientation, but also in how they express their masculinity. And yet they share a grand commonality—each one's quality of life is rooted in serving others.

Mentoring is service. It is nonjudgmental, tolerant, and aligned to humanitarian and spiritual principles. This approach allows space for young men to explore their masculinity, while simultaneously helping them develop skills and behaviors that lead to not only successful lives, but beautiful ones as well. Centered in mentorship is gratitude for learning how to live a beautiful life. The mentor is grateful for the opportunity to pass on the gifts that were given to him, and the mentee is grateful for those gifts, to the point that they then freely pass them on to the following generations. **A legacy of freely serving others then naturally becomes a part of man's identity, and it's the part that men need most to grow.**

"Let's Go for a Walk"

2000–Present

The Recruit

My wife Marissa and I first met when I was seventeen years old.

I left my hometown of Berwyn, PA, to visit Amherst College as one of their sport recruits. My host was a nice guy named Josh who took me to a basketball party on campus to say hello to a former teammate of mine (Andy) who had graduated from our high school two years earlier and was now playing on the Amherst men's basketball team.

I was six foot four, but being at a party with both the men's and women's basketball teams, I had never felt so short in my life. I was surrounded by older, larger, and more intelligent people. It was fairly intimidating.

Being naturally introverted, I looked for a corner spot where I'd be out of the mix and not make a fool of myself while still being able to see everyone. I sipped a beer that my host gave me and basically kept to myself, occasionally chatting with a few of the older male players who took an interest in me and wanted to represent the school. They were all nice, which helped me feel more comfortable.

My host moved around the party, encouraging me to engage people every ten minutes or so. Following his suggestion, I made an effort to talk to people, knowing it wasn't a strength of mine. Then, I saw her.

She was a six-foot-tall Minnesotan with long dirty blond hair, big, beautiful brown eyes, and the most gorgeous smile that I had ever seen. I sat down on a chair and could not take my eyes off her.

She saw me looking at her and started walking over to me. I choked on my beer immediately. As she got closer, I tried to think of what to say, but my brain wasn't working. I wanted to run away but I was frozen to the spot. With her long legs she walked across the entire room before I could gather myself. Suddenly, she was right next to me. I was a deer in headlights.

She said, "Hello."

I was struck mute. I couldn't say anything.

The party was incredibly loud. She got close to me, to the point that I could feel her breath on my ear, and asked, "It's too loud. Do you want to go for a walk?"

I got goose bumps and involuntarily blurted out, "Ihaveagirlfriend."

She replied with, "Okay?"

I was cursing myself in my head. I very much wanted to go for a walk with her, but I had no idea why I said that. Missing that walk would haunt me for the next decade.

That's how my wife and I first met. To date, it remains a running joke amongst my wife's friends who witnessed the hilariously awkward first encounter. Some still call me "The Recruit."

"I'm Not Interested in That"

The next day when I asked my host for Marissa's email, he laughed. I found out later that Marissa had asked him for mine as well.

Marissa and I got married fourteen years after we first met. However, we never dated during those long years because we were always many states apart and neither of us was interested in dating long distance (despite the fact that we were crazy about each other). We met in person a handful of times, but the vast majority of those years was spent communicating digitally. We logged thousands of emails and texts, and I can't even count how many hours we spent talking on the phone. We knew each other to the core and kept our friendship confidential. It felt sacred in its own way.

Although we shared a once-in-a-lifetime connection, there were several gaps that we just couldn't bridge. She found certain aspects of my lifestyle and identity to be intolerable and would not concede or compromise her values. She couldn't understand how I could be respectful of women but also sexually promiscuous. Nor could she understand how I could express my thoughts but be closed off emotionally. She asked me, "Why do you have to be that way?"

I respected her commitment to her values and didn't take it personally at all. I tried to explain to her that those traits were *just part of being a man,* and her response was, **"I'm not interested in that."**

That was our impasse.

Inevitably, we chose to stop talking to each other. She wasn't willing to accommodate those ideologies, and although I wanted to change, **I didn't know any other way** to be. We were both heartbroken and our final words to each other were, "I'm sorry. I love you."

We didn't speak for years. During that time, I took the service-based job at CITRS, was mentored by Gene and Brendan, started the consulting job, began working with the Angels, and was introduced to the "daughter standard" by Jeanne, which evolved into love and compassion for everyone.

I had given up all hope of us being together and accepted reality. **I missed my chance to be with her.**

"Thank You for Telling Me"

Marissa and I didn't exchange a single word for years. Then on a sunny day while I was sitting with my dad discussing plans for the future, my phone buzzed. I saw that I had an email. It was from *her*.

The world stopped spinning.

I waited until later that night to read it when I knew there was no chance of any distractions. While reading, I could hear her voice and it was a surreal experience. I read it at least ten times and then slept on it before replying late the following evening.

We scheduled a call after a few days and talked for hours. She was the same as she had always been, but wiser, more mature, and with more life experience, while I had become a different person. Fortunately, all the trust we had built in the past was stronger than ever in the present, but it still felt like we were starting over. We had a lot of ground to cover to learn what had happened in each other's lives since we last spoke.

This time I spilled my guts. I shared everything about myself including the events with my mother, the emotional complexities associated with attempting to renounce toxic male beliefs, and my difficulties integrating a new, evolving belief system. It took dozens of incoherent, sloppy, and emotional conversations. I imagine each one was a bit more than she bargained for, but she listened intently and fielded the conversations gracefully. After each one she'd say, **"Thank you for telling me."** That was it.

She didn't emasculate me. She didn't question my toughness or commitment. She didn't think I was any less of a man by expressing myself. She didn't do any of the things that society had led me to believe would paint a picture of me being "weak" in her eyes. It was the final piece necessary for both of us to move forward—authenticity and vulnerability.

We were finally ready to meet.

"I Gotta Go"

Although we couldn't wait to meet, we weren't in a rush either. It had been over seven years since the last time we saw each other, and life had swamped our calendars. I was consulting during the week and personal training on the weekends. She was trying to get her equestrian therapy practice up and running. We were both busy, so we pushed out our date to meet roughly two months down the road, but that didn't last.

It was a Friday and I was getting my first quarterly review from my new boss in northern New Jersey, just outside of New York City. The meeting basically consisted of constructive criticism. Although I had done well, I had made a few mistakes internally. They weren't a big deal in comparison to the revenue I generated, but the mistakes needed to be fixed for efficiency reasons. It was a positive but serious meeting.

Halfway through, I got a text from Marissa. She was visiting her Amherst friends in Connecticut, but her plane got grounded in New York City before she could get back to Minnesota on account of a nasty storm.

I asked my boss, "Do we need the whole hour?"

He said, "No, we're good if you understand."

"I understand."

"Okay good. Anything for me?" he asked.

"Nope. I gotta go."

He started laughing and asked, "Oh yeah? What's the rush? Does she have a name?"

By the time the words left his mouth, I was already out the door, in my car, and driving north in a torrential downpour. A distance that should've taken thirty minutes to complete lasted for almost four hours of white-knuckle driving. The traffic was terrible, and there were rain-related accidents everywhere. I was soaked in stress sweat.

I finally got to the hotel where she was staying. I had so many conflicting thoughts and emotions as she was walking toward me, but they all washed away when we got close.

She said, "Hello."

I didn't say anything and just hugged her. She hugged me back.

Our life together began that very moment.

What Really Matters

Marissa and I moved in together in Philly before moving back to Minnesota, which is where we got married and had two children, Tommy (four) and Bella Mae (two). We are a tightly knit family and nothing is better than being together. I am aware of how easily things could've *not* worked out, and I try to steep myself in gratitude every day for the providence that brought us together. It's a major incentive to continue exploring constructive masculine ideologies. Without me practicing empathy, spirituality, and humanity, Marissa would not have budged. She stood firm, and I have always admired her for that.

However, the toxic male beliefs of my former life still echo in my head. I see those beliefs alive and well in society. Even though they manifest pain in people's lives, they remain prevalent and persuasive.

Knowing that, I choose to check myself regularly and make sure that I'm keeping the proper perspective that always allows me to "put first things first." That's how I center myself and don't get derailed. For me, it's about relationships.

My old life came to an end with the loss of my relationship with my mother, whom I still love deeply and think about every day. The pain of that personal tragedy led me on a journey to many different places where I met incredible people. And I changed.

Poetically, the transformation was necessary. Without it, I would not know this life. Marissa and I would have never gotten married, and I would not know my children whom I love in ways I can't describe.

I express my masculinity through faith, family, and service. It is the nucleus of who I am. I by no definition believe this is the only masculine identity, but it is the only masculine identity for me.

That, more than anything, is what I hope people can understand. This was *my* journey to masculinity. It is not meant to be replicated. **The road out** from toxic masculinity will always be individualized regardless of who walks it. And although we do have to walk our own path in life, we don't have to walk alone.

Marissa and I walk together every day.

Conclusion

Toxic masculinity is centered on the destructive belief that a man must go through life independently. It is upon this belief that all other toxic male ideologies are built—emotional suppression, the need for prestige, dominance and control, oppression of women, sexual promiscuity, violence, indifference to human suffering, and false toughness. All these ideologies influence men to live a life of self-imposed isolation and to not share themselves with others. Self-awareness is then perceived as unnecessary, and things like emotional intelligence, meaningful relationships, and spirituality become unattainable. As a result, men are closed off to the most fundamental element of health and happiness—connection.

Ironically, men's interpretation of toughness seen exclusively through self-reliance is what has ultimately left men weak, fragile, and aimless. As men, we do need to be tough, but we do not need to be alone. In fact, it is unwise and ineffective to take that approach. We do need to be able to get through storms, press through adversity, etc., but we are far stronger—our ability to endure increases drastically—when we are connected to ourselves, others, and a higher power. Therefore, in order for men to become truly *resilient*, toughness has to be reframed to include vulnerability, empathy, and compassion, which are essential to building meaningful relationships. Without these connection-promoting virtues, men suffer alone by following a code of silence. Mentors defy the code of silence by fostering connection. They model healthy interpersonal interaction by sharing themselves freely and responsibly with those they mentor. Because of this, mentors can make a great impact on the health of those they mentor by defying toxic masculinity's core belief that men must go through life alone. Mentors are nonjudgmental and allow young men to know that someone cares about them. They create safe environments for discussion and help promote self-awareness, empathy, and faith. Mentoring does not threaten, diminish, or discredit the value in autonomy; it magnifies the power of an individual by helping him open up to external energies, thereby naturally increasing his strength, resilience, and performance. This is especially relevant for young men.

When young men know that they are cared for and are given the opportunity to explore their identity and emotionality in a safe, caring environment, the value in pursuing toxic male ideologies diminishes organically. They no longer feel the need to dominate others, pursue empty accomplishments, or engage in self-destruction to feed their ego. They instead choose to hold themselves accountable to constructive behaviors because they understand there is a meaningful, substantive return associated with those behaviors as opposed to the hollow, fleeting, and damaging effects of toxic masculinity. Social status, prestige, and domination no longer hold water. Authenticity, purpose in life, and the value of relationships gain traction.

The choice to become a father is also impacted positively when men learn to be vulnerable, empathetic, and resilient. It allows them to choose to be a safe, compassionate, and warm presence in the lives of their children instead of a domineering figure that demands respect, attention, and admiration even if at the cost of their children's well-being.

When masculinity is aligned to humanitarian and spiritual principles, the value in connection builds and self-sustains. Competition becomes more about making one another better, instead of seeking to establish superiority at the expense of others. With ego being appropriately slotted, scarcity can be removed from the male psyche and replaced by an abundance mentality through which everyone may benefit.

In the end, all young men need a guide—a mentor—that helps them connect and embrace the beauty in life when we open up to external energies and give ourselves to the service of others. Through our ability to connect, we can redefine what it means to be a man, and leave this world a little better than we found it.

Acknowledgments

E ven after everything that I've experienced—all the failure, pain, and regret—I wouldn't change a single thing. I live a life that is beautiful to *me*, and its light comes from the relationships that I have made over my lifetime. I am *grateful* for all my relationships and feel it is important to directly thank those who have been previously mentioned.

The CITRS team of Gene Miller, Brendan Petersen, Jeanne Craft, and Clay Hamlin all played a huge role in my development. They provided me with an opportunity to work with thousands of people from diverse backgrounds and challenged me to connect with all of them on a human level. They helped me understand that an *individual's character and integrity* are paramount to build trusting relationships and in turn, be successful in *life*. I cherish these friendships.

I am thankful for Con Aquilante and the Angels. Our partnership started because Con looked me dead in the eye and told me, "No one can do what you do." His belief in me exceeded my own, and I would not have taken the risk to bring Invictus to Minnesota without Con's confidence.

While in Minnesota, four men have taken me under their wings and showed me the way: Glen Gunderson, Trent Tucker, Mark Moe, and Shawn Neel.

Glen Gunderson and I have gone on many walk-and-talks in Minnesota's stunning state parks, which have been nothing short of illuminating. Glen is a remarkable human being, highly accomplished businessman, and public servant. Glen welcomed me to Minnesota with open arms. It has been a pleasure building a wonderful friendship with him and mentoring his children. I look forward to connecting with him on many more hikes in this great state.

Trent Tucker and I enjoy grabbing breakfast at the famous Good Day Café. He shares stories from his career as a professional basketball player in the NBA and tenure as a public servant of inner-city children, all of which blow my mind. He shows adamant dedication to treating everyone with kindness and humility. We have become good friends, and I always feel grateful to see "breakfast with Trent" on my calendar.

Mark Moe and I grab coffee regularly. Mark's experience as a lawyer, investor, entrepreneur, and philanthropist have made our conversations comprehensive. We talk about everything from business structuring and conflict management to religion and life philosophy. Many of my brightest career moments in Minnesota can be traced back to a conversation over coffee with Mark. Our friendship has been a blessing, and I am so grateful to have been given the opportunity to mentor his children.

After moving to Minnesota, the powers-that-be saw fit to have me cross paths with a therapist named Shawn Neel. There was a connection right away, but I could have never expected our relationship to turn into what it did. Shawn was the ultimate "safe space" and perfectly exemplified nonjudgmental guidance. Words cannot describe the extent to which he helped me *grow through the storm*. I would not be who I am without him, and I am thankful.

My sense of gratitude reaches new levels when I think

about my parents. Although we had to say goodbye, I feel grateful every day for the wonderful relationship that my mother and I shared for over twenty years. When I think of the word "kindness," I think of her and the lessons she shared with me regarding how important it is to treat everyone with respect. I carry those lessons with me every day. I keep her close to my heart and extend myself to others through her example.

My father and I are closer than ever before, especially now that I have a son and daughter. *Kids have a funny way of turning their grandfathers into boys and their fathers into men.* He has endured so many trials and tribulations, and it brings me great joy to see him be so happy with his grandchildren. I can't even begin to describe the impact he has made on me, nor can I describe how appreciative I am for the positive fatherly example he set in the face of tremendous hardship. If I end up being half the father he was to me, I'll consider my life a success. I wish that anyone going through a tough time could have the chance to speak to him. The world would be a better place.

I am grateful for my wife, Marissa. She is a remarkable human being, friend, partner, and co-parent. She has taught me countless lessons about empathy and human nature that have made me a better mentor, husband, father, and man. I would be lost without her. She is my saving grace. I love her.

About the Author

JOHN D'AGOSTINI graduated from the University of Pennsylvania, served in the Army, and led product development for a curriculum company prior to founding Invictus Leadership, a mentoring program. As the sole operator, John has helped hundreds of clients become successful as professional athletes, Olympians, Eagle Scouts, scholars, musicians, entrepreneurs, and purposeful, healthy human beings. He lives in Minnesota with his wife and two children and continues to mentor young men with unique goals from all backgrounds. John is available for speaking, consulting, and connecting at www.johndagsmentors.com.